THE STRATEGIC **UX** Toolkit

THE STRATEGIC **UX** Toolkit

Context-Driven Research and Design for EdTech

Kelly Morgan, Ph.D.

First Printing, 2026

ISBN: 978-0-9862971-2-0 (eBook)

ISBN: 978-0-9862971-3-7 (Print)

Kelly Morgan Strategic UX LLC

Colorado Springs, CO 80908

www.kellymorganux.com

DEDICATION

To all the teachers that just want tools work for them – I see you!

CONTENTS

INTRODUCTION

Why Strategic UX Thinking Matters More Than Any Framework

I've watched this happen too many times.

A product leader discovers Design Thinking at a conference. Or reads about Continuous Discovery on a blog. Or hears that Jobs-to-Be-Done transformed some successful company's approach to product development.

They come back energized. "This is it. This is what we need. If we just follow this framework, we'll finally build products that teachers and students love."

Six months later? The enthusiasm has faded. The framework didn't appear to deliver. Research insights sit unused. The team concludes "These formalized frameworks aren't worth it—we know what our users need" and moves on.

Here's the thing: The frameworks aren't bad. The context mismatch is the problem.

I've been on both sides of this failure. As a high school chemistry and physics teacher for fifteen years, I watched EdTech companies build products that looked great in demos but added friction to my already-impossible workload. Even when products were "research-backed" and "user-centered," they failed in real classrooms.

As a founding designer at multiple EdTech companies (non-profit, for-profit, government, and military contractor)—where I came in to build UX functions from scratch in mature companies—I've seen fantastic product teams struggle because they're applying frameworks designed for completely different contexts.

The issue isn't always that EdTech teams lack UX knowledge (sometimes it is, but definitely not always!). It's that EdTech doesn't align with the assumptions those frameworks make.

Standard UX frameworks assume:

- You can launch when you're ready
- Users can switch products if they're unhappy
- You can talk to users whenever you need insights
- Buyers and users are the same people
- Iteration improves trust

In EdTech, none of that is true.

You have immovable back-to-school deadlines. Teachers are locked in for nine months once school starts. User access can be seasonal. Admins buy, teachers control adoption, and students are end users with zero choice. Mid-year changes destroy trust instead of building it.

These aren't minor contextual differences. They're fundamental misalignments that confound standard approaches.

My Ph.D. in innovative instructional technology taught me how our brains think and learn, and how that understanding intersects with UX design. My years in the classroom taught me the brutal reality of teacher time poverty, cognitive load, and workflow constraints. My experience building UX functions at EdTech companies taught me how to navigate organizational history and politics, regulatory compliance, and technical debt while still delivering outcomes that matter.

What I learned: Strategic thinking matters more than any single framework.

The teams that succeed aren't the ones following frameworks most closely. They're the ones who understand their context deeply enough to know which tools to use—and when.

That's what this book provides.

What You'll Learn

Part 1: The Problem walks you through why standard UX frameworks don't always fit in EdTech:

- Chapter 1 details EdTech's unique constraints—timing cycles, lock-in periods, regulatory requirements, and technical debt— that break framework assumptions.
- Chapter 2 shows six specific framework misalignments and their real costs (why pre-built toolboxes don't fit EdTech).
- Chapter 3 explores the three-user dynamic where buyers, gatekeepers, and end users have different goals and control.
- Chapter 4 introduces six strategic principles for building your own toolkit instead of following pre-built frameworks.

Part 2: The Solution teaches you how to build The Strategic UX Toolkit—your own collection of methods selected for your specific EdTech constraints:

- Chapter 5 introduces the five-phase toolkit-building process.
- Chapter 6 (Phase 1): Assessing your context so you know which tools fit your reality.
- Chapter 7 (Phase 2): Selecting research tools and artifacts strategically based on your context.
- Chapter 8 (Phase 3): Executing research and building stakeholder buy-in using your selected tools.
- Chapter 9 (Phase 4): Developing a UX strategy and advocating for strategic direction.
- Chapter 10 (Phase 5): Designing solutions and advocating for prioritization.

This isn't another pre-built toolbox to follow rigidly. It's a strategic approach for building *your* toolbox by choosing methods that fit *your* specific constraints, timeline, and organizational reality.

Who This Book Is For

For founders and executives: This book offers strategic guidance for building UX capability from scratch in EdTech environments. You'll understand what "good UX" actually means in constrained contexts and how to evaluate whether your teams are making strategic decisions about which tools to use.

For product managers: Discover frameworks for assessing your context and selecting research methods strategically. Learn how to scope research to your actual constraints—calendar windows, budget realities, roadmap flexibility—instead of aspirational "best practices."

For UX leads and researchers: Build credibility and prove ROI in environments where standard approaches don't work. Learn which tools from various frameworks work in EdTech contexts, when to adapt them, and when to create custom approaches.

For designers: Understand the context your users actually operate in, not just teachers' workflows, but the systems, mandates, and pressures that constrain their choices. Learn which design tools help you design for the real world, not ideals.

You don't need to work in EdTech to benefit from this book. If you're working in any constrained, regulated, multi-stakeholder environment—healthcare, government, enterprise software, financial services—the strategic thinking tools transfer.

How to Use This Book

Read Part 1 first. Even if you're tempted to skip to the "how-to" in Part 2, don't. Understanding *why* frameworks fail is essential to making strategic decisions about which tools to use when.

Don't try to apply everything at once. This book teaches you to build your own toolkit by selecting methods that fit your context. Start with the constraints that matter most in your situation—maybe it's seasonal user access, maybe it's technical debt, or maybe it's three-user dynamics. Let your context guide which tools you select first.

Adapt, don't adopt. I'm not prescribing you a new framework to follow without question. I'm teaching you to assess your reality and select tools strategically, whether those tools come from Design Thinking, Continuous Discovery, JTBD, or custom approaches you design. Take what fits, modify what doesn't, and build your own toolkit for your specific situation.

Use the examples. Throughout the book, I share real examples from my work—what worked, what failed, and why. These aren't theoretical scenarios. They're battle scars from building UX functions in EdTech companies. My mistakes have paved a path to which tools work in which contexts. All you have to do is take my lessons learned and apply them to your own unique situations.

A Note on Frameworks

Let me be clear about something before we dive in: **I'm not anti-framework.**

Design Thinking, Continuous Discovery, Jobs-to-Be-Done, and Lean UX are brilliant methodologies created by thoughtful practitioners. I've learned from each of them and use tools from all of them.

The problem isn't the frameworks themselves. The problem is applying frameworks prescriptively without asking: "Does my reality match the reality this framework was designed for?"

When EdTech teams adopt frameworks without that assessment, research efforts fail. Not because the frameworks are bad, but because the context assumptions don't match.

This book teaches you to think strategically about context first, then select tools that fit, whether they come from established frameworks, are adapted versions, or are custom approaches you design for your specific constraints.

Think of frameworks as pre-built toolboxes. The goal isn't to reject them—it's to understand which tools fit *your* work, and to build your own toolkit from the best of them.

What This Book Isn't

- **This isn't a comprehensive guide to user research methods**. There are excellent books on interview techniques, usability testing, survey design, and analytics. I won't duplicate that content.
- **This isn't a step-by-step implementation guide with templates and worksheets**. Every EdTech company has different constraints, maturity levels, and resources. This book teaches you strategic thinking about tool selection. The Strategic UX Toolkit Playbook (available at kellymorganux.com) provides tactical implementation guides for using specific tools.
- **This isn't a criticism of frameworks or their creators**. They built excellent tools for the contexts they work in. I'm showing you when those contexts match EdTech reality and when they don't, so you can make informed decisions about which tools to use.

The Promise

By the end of this book, you'll be able to:

- Assess your specific EdTech constraints and how they impact which tools will work.
- Build your own strategic UX toolkit by selecting methods based on your context.
- Choose when to use tools from existing frameworks.

- Build stakeholder buy-in, so research actually drives decisions.
- Prove research ROI even in constrained environments.

You'll stop fighting frameworks that don't fit your context.

You'll start building your own toolkit and making strategic UX decisions that actually drive change.

Ready? Let's begin with why EdTech complicates everything you know about UX.

CHAPTER 1

Why EdTech Complicates What You Know About UX

"In theory, theory and practice are the same. In practice, they are not." — **Albert Einstein**

The Framework Trap

Remember that manager, director, or VP I mentioned in the intro? The one who comes to you with a life-changing blog post, podcast episode, or book? They've just discovered the solution to all the company's product problems. They are convinced that if everyone just follows this new framework, things will turn around. Not only that, but the team will create a product users can't live without.

More likely, this "newly discovered" framework will trigger endless meetings to co-create visuals for how it'll all be implemented, align workflows and ownership, circle back, take it offline, and then ... put a pin in it. That domino effect from the new shiny framework creates all the corporate theater that drives you crazy because you could have been doing actual work that made a difference.

And to be totally honest, none of what they brought to you is "new." If you're a product or UX professional, you've likely already read about this "new" framework they're introducing. At their core, all these frameworks are variations on the same two things: (1) understand what your users really, actually, truly need, and (2) spend the time to design-test-iterate until it's so seamless and intuitive that users can't remember what they did before.

That's it. That's the secret to building a great product.

Now, doing those two things—understanding what users really, actually, truly need and then design-test-iterating until it's amazing—is really hard. And that's where UX frameworks come in. But there's no single framework that does it all and works in every context. That's why having someone bring you the "latest and greatest" thing they just read—with expectations that everyone will adopt it completely and the product will magically transform—can be extremely exasperating.

UX frameworks are great. I've learned something valuable from each one I've studied. **The problem comes with rigid adoption.**

Adopting one doesn't mean throwing out pieces from others that have been working. Reading about a framework new to you doesn't mean people in your organization weren't already incorporating components of it. None of the frameworks will magically solve all your problems. And going "all in" on the latest blog post or book a manager has read is likely going to drive everyone a little crazy.

Every popular UX framework assumes a reality that doesn't exist in education. They assume you can launch when you're ready. They assume users can switch products when they're unhappy. They assume you can talk to users whenever you need to.

In EdTech? None of that is likely true.

Which is why I advocate learning from all the frameworks, creating a toolbox of methods, and deeply understanding your context to know which tools to pull out. "Right tool for the job," as my mom taught me.

EdTech is Different

I've been on both sides of this problem—as a teacher frustrated by EdTech products, and as a UX designer watching teams struggle to build them.

The issue is often that teams are applying frameworks designed for completely different constraints.

Let me walk you through what I mean.

Timing Constraints: The Sales Window You Can't Control

The Adoption Window Is Everything

Consumer products can be adopted at any time. B2B SaaS launches when the product is ready. EdTech? You have a window, and if you miss it, you wait a year.

Here's the typical pattern (give or take, depending on the area of the country):

- **February–June:** Adoption season. Schools evaluate tools, districts finalize purchases, and teachers get to try new products during professional development.

- **July–September:** Implementation crunch. Everyone's getting classrooms operational, training on new tools, and trying to survive the back-to-school chaos.
- **October–May:** Lock-in period. Teachers are drowning. They have zero bandwidth for new tools or major changes.

What this means for research: If you conduct brilliant research in February and discover what teachers need, you've missed the window. By the time you build and launch, it's September—too late for adoption decisions. You're going to have to wait until the *following* April.

And even if your Go To Market and Sales teams are promoting what *will* be released during adoption season, if you don't release (with documentation and training to support it) before the implementation crunch, it's too late. Educators will have already trained on the old version and don't have time to learn the new release. (You've also lost trust with internal teams, buyers, and users).

Your insights are now fourteen-plus months old before users will be implementing them.

Most UX frameworks assume you're in control of timing. In EdTech, the calendar controls you.

Lock-In Periods Mean You Can't Iterate Like Normal

When a consumer hates a product, they switch. Immediately. Cancel subscription, download competitor, problem solved.

Teachers can't do that.

When a district adopts a tool in July, teachers are locked in until at least the following June. Even if the product is frustrating. Even if it adds to their workload instead of reducing it. Even if they hate it.

They're stuck.

This fundamentally changes what "minimally viable" means.

In startup land, a minimally viable product (MVP) is something barely functional that you ship quickly to get feedback. If users don't like it, they leave, and you iterate based on what you learn. They might even come back to try again if they haven't found something else and see your improvements.

In EdTech, if teachers don't like your product in September, they spend nine months resenting it and planning their escape the moment June arrives. You don't get to iterate and win them back—the damage is permanent.

When users can't leave, what frameworks call "rapid learning" becomes "permanent trust damage."

The Back-to-School Deadline Is Immovable

Most products launch whenever they're ready. EdTech products face a hard deadline: School starts in August or September, depending on your state. Launch in October? Teachers are already overwhelmed managing 150 students, differentiating instruction, grading assignments, attending meetings, communicating with parents, and dealing with whatever crisis erupts that week.

They don't have the bandwidth to learn your new interface or adapt to workflow changes. They barely have bandwidth to get through the day. If you're launching a new feature or redesigning a workflow, it needs to be ready *before* school starts—ideally in July when teachers have time during professional development. Miss that window, and you're essentially launching to an audience who can't engage with what you built.

Continuous Discovery and Lean UX encourage ongoing iteration, but EdTech requires you to cluster changes around the calendar, whether your sprint schedule aligns with that or not. This doesn't mean you can't test-iterate, just that you shouldn't launch-iterate in your production environment.

Mid-Year Changes = Cognitive Disruption

Once teachers learn your workflow for the school year, changing it in November, even to make it "better," is perceived as disruptive. They've just spent two months building muscle memory, creating workarounds, and figuring out how to power through. Now you want them to relearn? They don't have time for that. And they likely don't trust that your "fix" actually *fixed* things since it didn't work right the first time around.

I've seen companies ship improvements mid-year that genuinely saved time for teachers. But, adoption *dropped* because teachers perceived the change as adding work (the cognitive load of relearning) rather than reducing it. The only changes teachers will tolerate mid-year are bug fixes and minor improvements that don't alter core workflows. Everything else waits until the next back-to-school launch. This breaks the "build-measure-learn" cycle that Lean UX depends on. You can't do weekly iterations during the school year without risking utilization drop-off.

The Beta Tester Trap

"We'll just use beta testers," teams say. "We'll partner with teachers who understand we're iterating, who thrive in co-design environments and fast iteration cycles." And yes, some educators love that process. They get excited about shaping the product. They're patient with rough edges because they see their feedback driving real improvements.

Problem solved, right?

Not quite.

Here's what actually happens: Beta testers get the benefit of knowing you're listening. They see their frustrations acknowledged and fixed. They understand the workarounds are temporary. Everyone else? They're stuck with the rough version for the entire school year. They don't know improvements are coming. They don't feel heard. They just know this product makes their job harder, and they spend nine months resenting it.

By the time the improved version launches the following year, the damage is done. Teachers have already decided your product isn't worth the hassle. They've already warned colleagues to avoid it. Even when you show them the better version, they remember how the first experience felt.

> Beta testing solves your iteration problem. But it doesn't solve your trust problem with the 95 percent of users who aren't in the beta program.

Access Constraints: You Can't Talk to Users When You Need To

User research is always challenging. Stakeholders question its value, budgets are tight, representative samples are elusive, and unmoderated tests are convenient but don't allow follow-up or course correction. EdTech takes these universal challenges and adds a whole new level of frustration.

Teachers Might Be Available Seasonally

Continuous Discovery assumes you can talk to users weekly. Jobs-to-Be-Done assumes you can recruit participants when needed. Lean UX assumes you can test throughout development. (More details on these frameworks in Chapter 3, in case you're not familiar!) In EdTech, teacher access is seasonal. So are their memories. You may be lucky and find teachers are available year-round, but if they haven't rostered students in six months, they're not going to remember last fall's rostering process in enough detail to give you effective feedback.

September–May: Teachers are slammed. They're teaching five classes, grading 150 assignments, writing lesson plans, managing student crises, communicating with parents, and preparing for state tests. Even if they want to help with research, they literally don't have time.

Reaching out during this period often feels tone-deaf. You're asking overwhelmed people to donate scarce free time (even if you have incentives!) to help you build a better product.

June–August: Teachers have capacity. Summer professional development, planning time, and actual availability for hour-long conversations. The gap? You get 10–12 weeks to gather insights that need to last an entire year.

"Weekly discovery interviews" becomes "summer research intensive followed by analytics-driven decisions when you can't access teachers." And even then, it can be hard to get in touch with many teachers. A significant portion, quite understandably, logs off during their break. They won't see your email, won't want to think about work, will be doing other professional development activities, and so on.

It's not about teachers being unwilling. It's about the fundamental reality of their work cycle.

Student Research Is a Regulatory Gauntlet

Think accessing teachers is hard? Try accessing students.

Students are minors (in K–12), which means research with them requires:

IRB approval: It can take 3–6 months if you don't have standing institutional approval (if necessary for the state or district you're working with).

Parental consent: This is a rolling administrative burden because parents need to opt in, and forms should be in multiple languages.

District permission: Often requires board approval, superintendent sign-off, and political considerations.

School-level approval: You need principal buy-in, teacher cooperation, and scheduling around instruction.

Even after clearing these hurdles, you can only observe students during the school year when they're actually in classrooms—and classroom observation is logistically complex, potentially disruptive, and politically sensitive.

What frameworks call "continuous validation" becomes "plan research six months ahead and hope your questions are still relevant."

I've been in companies where they skip these steps. They equate "school/teacher permission to *observe* in a classroom" with "permission to *talk* with students." And even when they do have specific permission to talk with students, they skip the parental permission piece. This opens the company up to liability issues. I strongly advise—at all costs—to not shortcut the process of securing permission to talk with students.

Political and Regulatory Reality: Compliance Isn't Optional

The 12–18 Month Approval Process

Some states and large districts maintain approved vendor lists. If you're not on the list, schools can't purchase your product. It doesn't matter that teachers love it; it solves their exact problem; and your pricing is better.

Getting approved requires:

- Demonstrating FERPA compliance
- Proving data security meets state standards
- Showing accessibility conformance (Section 508, WCAG)
- Documenting student data privacy practices
- Waiting 12–18 months for the approval cycle

- Making it through the gauntlet of politics, relationships, firmly held beliefs, and all the other things

You can't just research, build, and launch. You need to research, build in alignment with approval requirements (which sometimes change after you've started building), submit for approval, wait, and *then* launch.

Timeline planning in EdTech must account for political and regulatory reality, not just speed of development.

Regulatory Compliance Overrides UX Decisions

Consumer products optimize for user delight. EdTech products must optimize for user delight within mandatory regulatory constraints:

- **FERPA:** Student data privacy rules are strict about what data you can collect and share.
- **COPPA:** Children under thirteen require parental consent, and data collection is limited.
- **State-specific privacy laws:** You also have to comply with California's SOPIPA, New York's Ed Law 2-d, and dozens of others.
- **Section 508 and WCAG:** These impose accessibility standards that are *legally required* for public school procurement.

A team might design a beautiful solution that violates FERPA, an engaging feature that requires data that COPPA prohibits, or a workflow that isn't accessible to screen reader users—disqualifying you from procurement.

Compliance requirements must inform research from day one. You're not just asking "What do users need?" You're asking, "What do users need that we can legally and compliantly provide?"

Funding Sources Have Strings Attached

Consumer products are funded by revenue. B2B SaaS is funded by investors or revenue.

EdTech money comes from everywhere, and each source has different rules:

- **Federal grants** → specific features required, strict spending categories
- **State budgets** → aligned with state standards, procurement processes
- **District allocations** → subject to board approval, constrained by local policies
- **Title I funding** → serves specific student populations, restrictions on use
- **Technology grants** → hardware/software restrictions, integration requirements
- And so on ...

A framework might reveal that teachers need Feature X, but if Feature X doesn't align with grant requirements or state standards, you can't build it, even if it's the right solution. You can't just research user needs in a vacuum. You need to research user needs that can be funded within existing constraints. Otherwise, you'll generate solutions that die in budget meetings.

Technical and Organizational Reality: What You Can Actually Build

Legacy Systems Lock You In

Many established EdTech companies have decades of code. We're talking layers of technical debt. Platforms built before modern web standards. Integrations with external systems that dictate data structures. Research might reveal that teachers need a completely different workflow. But if implementing it requires rebuilding core platform architecture, that research insight sits unused.

I've experienced this on numerous occasions—a workflow that doesn't work for users, but we can't change it because if we touch thing A, it impacts thing B, which impacts thing C, and so on through twenty-plus years of decisions built upon decisions. Fixing it all (or often better, starting from scratch) is outside the bounds of your time or resources. Or it will take longer than the board is willing to wait for the results.

Before researching solutions, understand what's technically feasible. Don't spend three months discovering that teachers need something your platform fundamentally can't support without a multi-year rebuild. *Or* be prepared to present your findings in a way that will gain buy-in from stakeholders: that the multi-year rebuild is exactly what's needed for your product to survive. But come with phasing plans, cost and time estimates, return on investment, and user research data. No doubt, it's a hard battle, but sometimes it's the right one—and it pays off.

Roadmap Commitments Override User Research

Consumer startups can pivot based on user feedback. EdTech companies with enterprise customers have contractual commitments. When a state or large district signs a three-year contract that includes specific feature roadmap commitments (or freezes the product during their contract), you're locked in. Research that reveals a better direction doesn't matter if you're contractually obligated to build Features A, B, and C first, or prevented from changing D.

Understand roadmap flexibility before choosing research methods. If your roadmap is locked for twelve months, don't do generative research identifying new opportunities. Do evaluative research to improve what you're already committed to building.

Technical and organizational constraints shape what research you can do. But there's another layer of complexity that shapes who you should research in the first place.

Multi-User Complexity: Buyer ≠ Gatekeeper ≠ User

Most frameworks assume the buyer and user are the same person. Or that users voluntarily choose products.

EdTech doesn't follow these assumptions.

You have three distinct user types:

- **Admins** buy your product and control budgets.
- **Teachers** control whether students ever use what was purchased.
- **Students** use what teachers assign, whether they like it or not.

This creates a fundamental adoption problem: The people who buy your product (admins) aren't the people who control whether it gets used (teachers), and the people it's designed for (students) have zero choice.

When your admin portal has an NPS of 60 but your teacher portal has an NPS of 33, teachers won't use your product with students. It doesn't matter how brilliant your student content is.

We'll explore this dynamic in depth in Chapter 3—why teachers are the actual gatekeepers, what context they're operating in, and how designing for the wrong user kills adoption. For now, understand this: **Designing disproportionately for users who don't control adoption is a recipe for failure.**

The Most Dangerous Phrase in EdTech UX

"It's the way we've always done it."

(Closely followed by "Company X did it this way, so we should" and "I just read this book and it sounds great, let's go all in!")

Successful companies used frameworks that fit their context. Your context is likely different. Your context changes from one moment in time or one project to another.

What works brilliantly at Spotify (Continuous Discovery with weekly access to users who voluntarily chose their product) fails at EdTech companies, where users are seasonal, adoption is mandated, and lock-in periods prevent switching.

What works at IDEO (Design Thinking for clients with flexible timelines and greenfield problems) fails at EdTech companies with immovable August deadlines and fifteen years of technical debt.

What provides a home run now may not work at all next year when your context has shifted.

The solution isn't to abandon frameworks. It's to understand your context first, *then* select tools strategically.

The Strategic Questions That Matter

Instead of following frameworks blindly, EdTech teams need to start with context assessment.

Your sales cycle timing, roadmap commitments, user access patterns, technical constraints, regulatory requirements, and adoption dynamics fundamentally shape which research methods will actually work. A technique that's brilliant in one context becomes wasteful—or even harmful—in another.

This isn't chaos. It's strategic thinking: using the right techniques for your specific situation instead of dogmatically following one framework regardless of fit.

That's what The Strategic UX Toolkit provides: A way to assess your context and make informed decisions about which methods will actually work.

We'll explore this strategic, context-driven approach in depth in Part 2 of this book, walking through the complete toolkit with real examples. For now, understand that the alternative to a rigid framework application isn't abandoning structure. It's choosing a structure that fits your reality.

Moving Forward

You now understand why EdTech constraints break standard UX frameworks. Immovable deadlines, lock-in periods, seasonal access, regulatory requirements, technical debt, and multi-user complexity fundamentally change what "good UX practice" means.

Next, we'll examine specific framework misalignments. You'll see exactly how Design Thinking, Continuous Discovery, Lean UX, Jobs-to-Be-Done, Disruptive Research, and Object-Oriented UX break when applied to EdTech's unique constraints—and how to use them strategically instead of dogmatically.

CHAPTER 2

When Good Frameworks Aren't Right for Your Context

"When all you have is a hammer, everything looks like a nail." — ***Abraham Maslow***

"When all you have is Design Thinking, every problem looks like it needs a sprint." ***(adapted)***

The Real Problem Isn't the Frameworks

Remember: Design Thinking isn't bad. Jobs-to-Be-Done isn't bad. Continuous Discovery, Lean UX, Disruptive Research—none of these frameworks are inherently problematic. In fact, they're all valuable tools!

Every framework contains brilliant insights. Teresa Torres wonderfully explains how to ground interview questions in past experiences rather than hypotheticals, and the importance of product trios. Larry Marine and Debbie Levitt help teams recognize when they need disruptive versus iterative research. Bob Moesta explains the emotional and social dimensions of product adoption.

These aren't competing philosophies where you must choose sides. They're tools in a toolkit—and the best craftspeople know which tool to use when.

The misalignments I'm going to walk you through aren't about frameworks being wrong. They're about teams applying frameworks without understanding their own constraints first.

So as you read these six misalignment patterns, don't dismiss the frameworks. Instead, ask yourself: "What assumptions does this framework make about context? Do those assumptions match my reality?"

That's the shift from rigid framework application to strategic method selection.

Understanding the Framework Landscape

Before we dive into specific misalignment patterns, let's get clear on what we're actually talking about when we say "framework." Not all frameworks are created equal. They serve different purposes, were designed for different contexts, and answer different questions.

Four Types of Frameworks

Frameworks fall into four broad categories:

1. **Process Frameworks** tell you *how to work*—they provide steps, phases, or workflows for approaching research and design.

   They answer:

   - "What should we do first?"

- "How do we move from research to solutions?"
- "What's the sequence?"

Examples: Design Thinking, Continuous Discovery, Lean UX, Double Diamond, Design Sprints

2. **Research Frameworks** tell you *what to investigate*—they provide lenses for understanding users, problems, or behaviors.

They answer:

- "Why do people choose products?"
- "What motivates behavior?"
- "How do we discover unarticulated needs?"

Examples: Jobs-to-Be-Done, Disruptive Research, Fogg Behavior Model

3. **Structural Frameworks** tell you *how to organize*—they provide systems for structuring design artifacts, components, or information.

They answer:

- "How should we organize our design system?"
- "How do we think about object relationships?"

Examples: Object-Oriented UX (OOUX), Atomic Design, task-based design

4. **Design Principles & Laws** tell you *what makes interfaces usable*—they provide evidence-based guidelines for creating intuitive, efficient interactions.

They answer:

- "Why is this interface confusing?"
- "How do I reduce cognitive load?"
- "What makes this button hard to click?"

Examples: Nielsen Norman Group's 10 Usability Heuristics, Hick's Law, Fitts' Law, Miller's Law, Jakob's Law

Understanding which type of framework you're looking at helps clarify what it can and can't do. A process framework won't tell you how to organize your design system. A structural framework won't tell you when to do research. Design principles won't tell you whether to use Continuous Discovery or Design Thinking—but they'll help you evaluate whether your designs actually work once you build them.

Where These Frameworks Came From

Design Gets Systematic

Before the 2000s, design was treated as artistic intuition. User research existed but lived separately from design.

The UK Design Council introduced the Double Diamond in 2004, one of the first attempts to document design as a systematic process. Around the same time, IDEO was codifying its practices into what would become Design Thinking.

Human-Centered Design Goes Mainstream

IDEO formally introduced Design Thinking in the mid-2000s, positioning it as human-centered innovation accessible to non-designers. This methodology emphasized empathy, ideation, and rapid prototyping, and Stanford's d.school soon began teaching it. IDEO.org adapted these principles for social impact work, creating Human-Centered Design specifically for nonprofits and social enterprises working with underserved communities.

Meanwhile, Clayton Christensen's disruption theory led to Jobs-to-Be-Done with Bob Moesta in the late 2000s. Rather than focusing on demographics or feature requests, JTBD asked: "What job is the customer hiring this product to do?" and "What makes them switch from one product to another?"

Lean, Agile, Continuous Thinking, and Disruptive Research

As startups embraced Lean and Agile, design needed to adapt. Jeff Gothelf and Josh Seiden developed Lean UX around 2011–2013, bringing design thinking into rapid iteration cycles. The emphasis shifted from deliverables to outcomes.

Jake Knapp at Google Ventures developed Design Sprints as a compressed version of design thinking—solve problems and test solutions in five days.

Teresa Torres formalized Continuous Discovery in 2021, advocating for integrating research into weekly product development rather than treating it as a phase. The outcome-focused approach and opportunity solution trees provided elegant tools for maintaining shared understanding.

Larry Marine and Debbie Levitt published *Disruptive Research* in 2023, challenging teams to observe users in solution-agnostic contexts to discover category-defining opportunities instead of incremental improvements.

Structural Frameworks Emerge

Brad Frost introduced Atomic Design in 2013, bringing systematic thinking to design systems by breaking interfaces into fundamental building blocks (atoms, molecules, organisms, templates, pages).

Sophia Prater developed Object-Oriented UX in the mid-2010s, applying object-oriented programming principles to UX design. By mapping user mental models to object relationships, OOUX helps create clear information architecture in complex systems.

Behavioral Models Enter Design

BJ Fogg's Behavior Model (2007) provided a simple formula: Behavior = Motivation × Ability × Prompt. This gave designers a diagnostic tool for understanding why adoption fails. Nir Eyal's Hooked Model (2014) showed how to create habit-forming products through cycles of trigger, action, variable reward, and investment. Powerful for engagement, but ethically problematic when applied to children or vulnerable users.

Now that you understand where these frameworks came from and what problems they were designed to solve, let's look at what they have in common—and where they diverge in ways that matter for EdTech.

Where Frameworks Overlap

Despite their differences, most frameworks share core principles:

- **Empathy before solutions:** Nearly all frameworks emphasize learning about users before jumping to design. They differ in *how* to develop that empathy, but agree it comes first.

- **Iteration over perfection:** None advocate for waterfall "design it once, ship it, done." All embrace learning, testing, and refining, though they differ dramatically in when and how.
- **Validation through testing:** Every framework includes some version of "check your assumptions with real users," whether via usability testing, assumption testing, prototype validation, or experiments with live products.
- **Cross-functional collaboration:** Modern frameworks assume designers don't work in isolation. They emphasize involving product managers, engineers, stakeholders, and users throughout.
- **Outcome orientation:** Especially in newer frameworks (Continuous Discovery, Lean UX, JTBD), the focus has shifted from outputs (wireframes, mockups) to outcomes (learning, validated decisions, problems solved).

These commonalities mean you're not starting from scratch when moving between frameworks. The fundamentals translate—it's the context-specific application that changes.

Where Frameworks Diverge

But frameworks differ dramatically in ways that matter:

Framework Comparisons

- Design Sprints (DS)
- Jobs To Be Done (JTBD)
- Lean UX (LUX)
- Design Thinking (DT)
- Continuous Discovery (CD)
- Double Diamond (DD)
- Disruptive Research (DR)

Time to insights

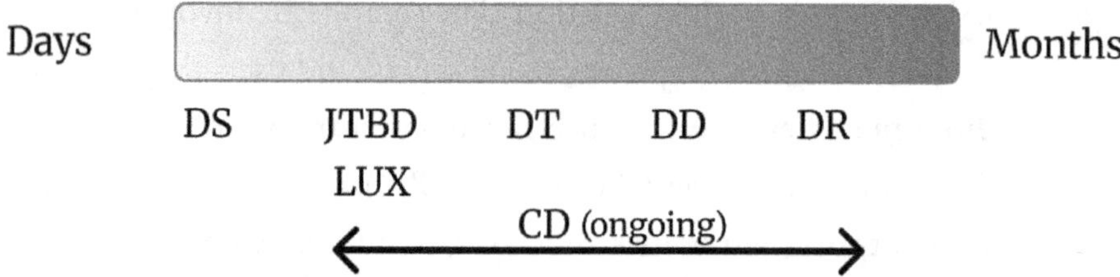

Research Depth

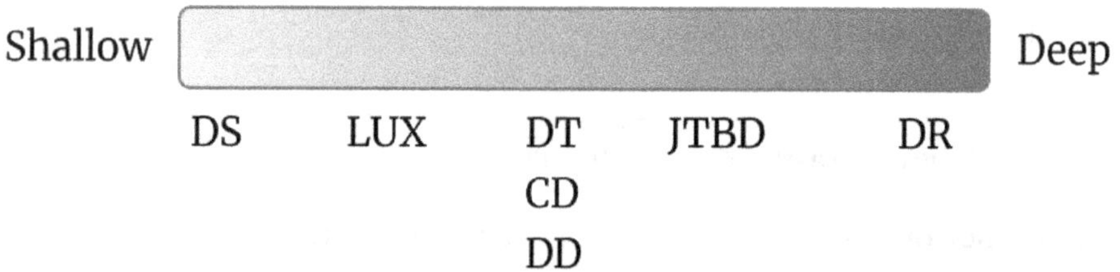

User Access Need

Compatibility with Technical Debt

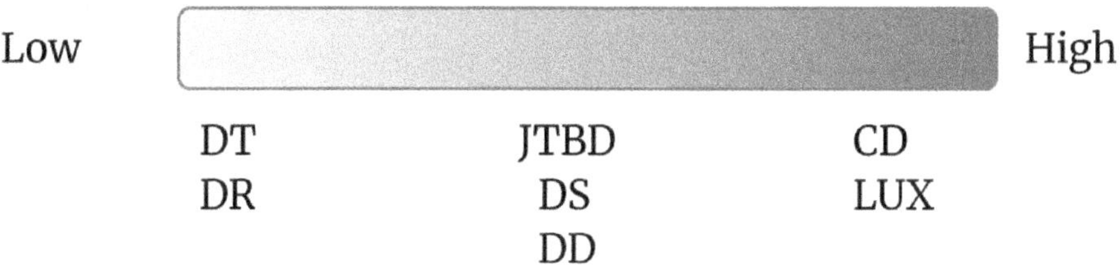

Organizational Maturity Required

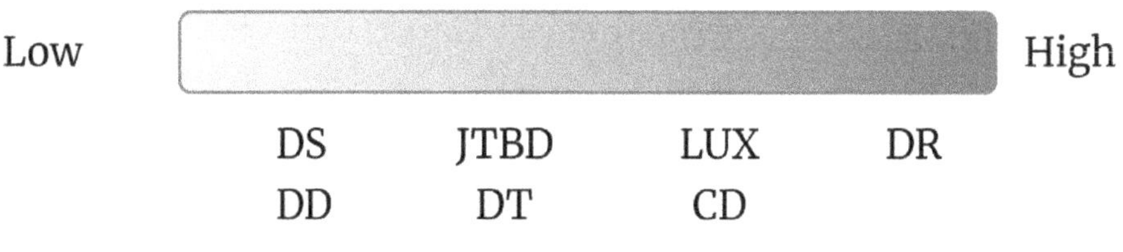

These differences aren't flaws—they're features. Each framework was designed for a specific context. The problem comes when teams ignore these differences and apply frameworks regardless of fit.

A Note on Behavioral Frameworks and Ethics

Before we move to specific patterns, a brief word about behavioral frameworks like Fogg's Behavior Model and the Hooked Model.

Fogg's Behavior Model is diagnostically useful. Understanding that behavior requires motivation, ability, and a prompt or trigger helps explain why adoption fails. If teachers aren't using your feature, you can diagnose by asking: Is motivation low? Is it too hard? Is the prompt missing or poorly timed?

This is valuable thinking.

The Hooked Model is more ethically fraught. It was designed to create habit-forming, potentially addictive products. Variable rewards, investment loops, and trigger optimization absolutely increase engagement. But when your users are children—or when you're designing learning tools where intrinsic motivation matters—manipulation-based engagement creates serious problems.

EdTech companies implementing Hooked Model tactics can have devastating results:

- Students are more motivated by badge-collecting than actual learning.
- Teachers complain that gamification replaces comprehension.
- Parents report addictive behaviors.
- District data privacy officers flag features that violate COPPA.

This doesn't mean behavioral thinking has no place in EdTech. Understanding what motivates teachers (efficiency, professional credibility, student outcomes) and what creates friction (training burden, cognitive load, workflow disruption) is essential.

But using manipulation-based engagement tactics on vulnerable users crosses ethical lines. I strongly suggest looking in the educational literature about motivation and the use of technology in learning rather than relying on consumer-based advice for increasing engagement. As a former educator, I believe the education literature is a far more ethical source of information.

As you read the following misalignment patterns, keep this ethical dimension in mind. Not all techniques that work should be used.

Six Ways Context Mismatches Waste Effort

Misalignment Pattern 1: Design Thinking → Innovation Without Execution Reality

What it is: Human-centered innovation emphasizing empathy, ideation, prototyping, and testing. Popularized by IDEO and Stanford's d.school.

What it gets right: The emphasis on empathy before solutioning is invaluable. Starting with deep user understanding, generating many potential solutions before choosing one, and prototyping to think through possibilities are all practices I use regularly.

<u>Where it breaks in EdTech:</u>

Scenario A: February Research, July Deadline Missed

An EdTech startup runs a Design Thinking sprint in January. Teachers love the validated prototype by Friday afternoon.

The problem? Engineering needs four months to build. That means the startup is launching in late May, *after* districts finalize purchasing for the next school year.

The insights were solid. The timing was unfortunate. They now have to wait until the *following* cycle, aging their research insights to over a year old before they can capitalize on them.

Why this happened: Design Thinking assumes you can launch when ready. EdTech has immovable sales cycles.

The question they should have asked: "When do decisions need to be made, and does our research timeline align with that window?"

Scenario B: Brilliant Solutions, Unbuildable Architecture

A company uses Design Thinking to reimagine its gradebook. Teachers love it in testing—it would save twenty minutes daily.

Implementation requires rebuilding core platform architecture. Engineering estimates eighteen months. With fifteen years of technical debt and enterprise customer commitments, leadership says no.

The insights sit in a Miro board, unused.

Why this happened: Design Thinking asks "What should we build?" without asking "What can we build given our constraints?"

The question they should have asked: "What's technically feasible, and should we research within those constraints?"

What Design Thinking still offers:

- Empathy-building exercises help teams understand users deeply.
- Ideation techniques generate creative solutions.
- Rapid prototyping allows testing before committing to development.

How to use it strategically:

Run Design Thinking sprints when you have time to build and launch by the deadline for the sales cycle or back-to-school launch. Or use empathy and ideation phases while consciously constraining prototyping to buildable solutions.

Misalignment Pattern 2: Jobs-to-Be-Done → Wrong User, Wrong Context

<u>Start with the problem:</u>

A company conducts JTBD interviews with teachers. Research reveals teachers want to "give feedback quickly while maintaining work-life balance." They design a gradebook optimized for teacher efficiency. Teachers love it in testing.

But admins aren't hiring gradebooks for teacher time-saving. They're hiring them to "ensure state reporting compliance" and "demonstrate accountability to the board." The product teachers love doesn't address the buyer's job. Purchasing decisions go to the company's competitors.

<u>The framework mismatch:</u>

Jobs-to-Be-Done, developed by Clayton Christensen and Bob Moesta, focuses on understanding the "job" people hire products to accomplish through functional, emotional, and social dimensions. Understanding that a teacher isn't just "looking for a gradebook" but "hiring a tool to reduce grading time while providing meaningful feedback" reveals design opportunities that demographic-focused research would miss. Purely functional analysis typically doesn't emphasize those emotional and social dimensions: "I want to feel like a good teacher" or "I don't want to look incompetent."

No doubt, JTBD leads to powerful thinking. But it assumes the user and buyer are the same person. EdTech has three users with different jobs.

<u>Another failure mode:</u>

A team asks students why they use their school's LMS. But students didn't hire anything—the district mandated it. Teachers didn't choose it either. It was selected three years ago by people who've since left.

The entire premise of JTBD—understanding "hiring" and "firing" moments—doesn't apply when adoption is involuntary. JTBD was designed for consumer contexts with voluntary adoption. EdTech often involves mandated tools with lock-in periods.

<u>Strategic use:</u>

Research the jobs of all three user types.

1. What job is the admin hiring your product to do?
2. What job is the teacher hiring it to do?
3. What job do students need it to do?

When adoption is involuntary, reframe the question from "Why did you hire this?" to "What would make this less of a burden?"

Misalignment Pattern 3: Continuous Discovery → Access You Don't Have

<u>What it does terrifically:</u>

Teresa Torres' Continuous Discovery gets outcomes right. Focus on what users need to accomplish, not what features to build. Ground interview questions in specific past experiences, not hypothetical futures. Use opportunity solution trees to maintain shared understanding across teams.

All of this dramatically improves research quality.

The problem? It assumes weekly user access.

<u>The seasonal reality:</u>

A product trio commits to weekly teacher interviews, with no budget for tools or staffing to facilitate the scheduling, and nothing available for teacher incentives (a reality I've lived). In June, it works beautifully—teachers have time, recruitment is easy. Or it doesn't work at all in June because you can't get any teachers willing to be online for free.

By October, the practice collapses. Teachers are drowning. Email outreach gets no responses. Those who do respond cancel because of crises: student behavioral issues, parent complaints, or unexpected testing mandates. Six weeks with no teacher contact, but product decisions still need to be made.

Meanwhile, another team wants weekly discovery interviews about the end-of-year rollover process. But it's currently February, and users have experienced a lifetime since they last completed those tasks. Their responses are likely to be best guesses rather than accurate descriptions.

<u>When organizational maturity isn't there:</u>

A founding UX designer tries to implement Continuous Discovery at a startup. Leadership loves research in theory, but deprioritizes it under pressure: "Can we skip interviews this week? We need you to design for the investor demo." After two months of inconsistent practice, it fades. The designer feels like they've failed.

Continuous Discovery requires a level of organizational commitment that many EdTech companies simply don't have. Research often gets sacrificed under shipping pressure.

Adapt, don't abandon: Use "continuous" to mean "as continuous as access allows." Batch intensive research during times when teachers are accessible, and their memory is fresh. Use analytics, existing recordings, and admin interviews during the school year. The interview techniques and opportunity mapping work beautifully even without a weekly cadence.

Misalignment Pattern 4: Lean UX → Speed Optimized, Trust Destroyed

<u>The promise and the trap:</u>

Lean UX brings bias toward action over endless planning. Learn from real usage. Build minimum viable products, test quickly, iterate based on feedback. The focus on learning from real usage grounds decisions in reality. The collaborative, cross-functional approach breaks down silos.

In consumer tech, this works because unhappy users leave immediately. Cancel subscription, download competitor, problem solved.

Teachers can't do that.

<u>What happens in practice:</u>

A startup ships a classroom management tool quickly, following Lean UX principles. It's minimally viable but clunky, adding ten minutes to teachers' daily workflows. In consumer tech, unhappy users leave immediately. In EdTech, teachers are locked in. They can't switch mid-year.

Nine months of resentment follow, and teachers start warning colleagues to avoid it.

The company iterates monthly based on usage data. Each iteration makes it objectively better—fewer clicks, clearer labels. But teachers hate it because every monthly update requires relearning. "I finally figured this out, and now you've changed it again." Utilization drops with each improvement.

When June arrives, teachers immediately switch to competitors. The startup never gets a chance to show improvements. That resentment-inducing first impression created permanent trust damage, and mid-year changes felt like instability rather than support.

Strategic use: Define "viable" based on EdTech lock-in reality: Users will live with your product for 9–12 months. Use rapid iterations with beta users or in usability testing with prototypes, not in production with all users. Batch workflow changes for summer releases.

Misalignment Pattern 5: Disruptive Research → Revolutionary Insights, Unbuildable Solutions

The fundamental tension:

Disruptive Research, developed by Larry Marine and Debbie Levitt, is designed to discover category-defining innovation through solution-agnostic observation. Watch how teachers accomplish tasks without your product (or any product) to reveal opportunities you'd never see by just studying existing tools. The emphasis on discovering problems rather than validating solutions prevents incremental improvement thinking.

It's brilliant thinking when you have:

- Greenfield contexts
- Runway for revolutionary products
- No technical debt
- Patient investors
- Political capital

Most EdTech companies have none of these.

Three ways revolutionary insights die:

1. **A company invests six months in Disruptive Research, observing teachers in analog contexts**. The insights are revolutionary: Teachers need something radically different from existing classroom management tools. But implementing the vision requires rebuilding the entire platform. Engineering estimates eighteen months minimum. Investors want revenue growth this quarter. The board rejects it. Research sits unused while the company continues incremental improvements.

2. **A team designs a completely new approach to formative assessment through Disruptive Research**. Teachers in testing love it. But it's not the way your organization has operated previously. You don't have the organizational UX maturity to break out of the boxes the company has built for itself.

3. **Research reveals teachers need seamless integration across five systems**: student information system, LMS, gradebook, communication platform, and an assessment tool. Building that requires partnership agreements with Google, Canvas, PowerSchool, and others. The startup has no existing relationships and no leverage to negotiate. The insight is spot-on, but the solution is impossible without partnerships, which take years to establish.

Strategic use: Use Disruptive Research selectively for strategic initiatives where you have the bandwidth to act—greenfield product development, major platform decisions. For incremental improvements, use iterative research revealing opportunities buildable within current constraints.

Misalignment Pattern 6: Object-Oriented UX → Beautiful Models, Regulatory Override

The conflict:

Sophia Prater's Object-Oriented UX maps user mental models to object relationships, creating clear information architecture from the bottom up. Understanding how users think about relationships between students, assignments, classes, and teachers prevents designs that match your technical model but confuse users. The focus on user mental models rather than database architecture creates more intuitive systems. The systematic approach to understanding object relationships prevents ad-hoc information architecture. Until regulatory requirements entirely override user preferences.

<u>Reality check:</u>

A team spends three months mapping teacher mental models using OOUX. They produce beautiful object diagrams showing how teachers think about Students, Assignments, Classes, and Assessments. When they try to get state approval, they learn that the state requires specific object structures for data integration. Their "Student" object has fifteen attributes based on teacher mental models. The state mandates forty compliance attributes that make no sense to teachers but are legally required. The team must choose: redesign and lose months of work, or don't get approved and lose the market.

Or they design intuitive object relationships that test well using OOUX, then discover that every student information system structures data differently. Their beautiful object model doesn't map to PowerSchool or Infinite Campus. They need transformation layers for each integration, adding months of complexity.

Strategic use: Document regulatory requirements and integration constraints alongside user mental models. Validate object models thoroughly before launch through prototyping. Use OOUX for greenfield development or major redesigns where you can establish constraints upfront, not incremental improvements where you're locked in.

The Pattern Behind All Six Misalignments

Notice what these misalignments have in common:

Context assumptions that don't match EdTech reality: Continuous access, voluntary adoption, flexible timelines, unconstrained innovation

Optimizing one dimension while ignoring others: User needs without technical constraints, innovation without political reality, speed without trust implications

Timeline expectations that ignore market dynamics: Research when convenient rather than aligned with sales cycles

Access assumptions that don't account for gatekeeping: Weekly interviews without seasonal barriers, student research without IRB

Risk tolerance that doesn't fit lock-in periods: MVP thinking when users can't exit for months

Political blindness to approval processes: Designing ideal solutions without regulatory constraints

The frameworks aren't bad. But teams applied them without understanding whether the client's context aligned with theirs

What These Misalignments Cost

These misalignments aren't theoretical. They have real consequences:

Wasted research effort. Months spent on research that can't influence decisions because timing is wrong, insights are unbuildable, or organizational maturity doesn't support the approach.

Missed market windows. Research completed in February can't influence July launches. Insights unused until next year will be outdated.

Lost credibility. UX leaders who push for frameworks their organizations can't support lose credibility when research doesn't drive decisions. "We tried UX research, and it didn't work" becomes organizational memory.

Damaged user trust. Products launched too early. Mid-year changes felt like instability to overwhelmed teachers.

Opportunity cost. Resources spent on approaches that don't fit could have been spent on methods that would drive decisions.

False conclusions. Teams concluding "frameworks don't work in EdTech" rather than "we need to assess the context before selecting frameworks."

The Alternative: Strategic, Context-Driven Selection

So if a rigid framework application doesn't work, what does?

A fundamental shift: Instead of asking "What's the best framework?" ask:

"What's our context, and which tools fit that context?"

This means understanding:

- **Organizational context:** UX maturity, roadmap flexibility, technical constraints, timeline pressure

- **EdTech-specific context:** Sales cycle stage, user access reality, lock-in implications, regulatory requirements, three-user dynamics

Then strategically combine techniques from multiple frameworks:

From Continuous Discovery: Interview techniques (grounding in past experiences), outcome focus, opportunity mapping, product trio work. Adapt "weekly" to your access windows.

From Disruptive Research: Solution-agnostic observation when you need breakthrough insights and have time to act. The distinction between disruptive and iterative research.

From JTBD: Emphasis on emotional and social dimensions, focus on motivations. Adapt "hiring" for involuntary adoption.

From Lean UX: Bias toward action and learning from usage. Redefine "minimum viable" for lock-in periods and task seasons.

From Design Thinking: Empathy-building exercises and ideation. Align research time with market windows.

From OOUX: Systematic approach to object relationships. Start with regulatory or integration constraints alongside user mental models.

This isn't framework chaos. It's strategic selection—taking the best from each based on what your situation demands.

That's what The Strategic UX Toolkit provides: not another framework to apply without question, but a way to assess your context and make informed decisions about which techniques will actually work.

Moving Forward

You now understand how popular frameworks fail when applied without context assessment. Six common misalignment patterns waste research effort, damage credibility, and lead teams to conclude "UX research doesn't work here."

Next, we'll examine the three-user dynamic in depth. You'll see why teachers are the actual gatekeepers, what context they're operating in, and how over-indexing on the wrong user kills adoption.

CHAPTER 3

Why Your Brilliant Student Features Aren't Getting Used

*"If a tree falls in a forest and no one is around to hear it, does it make a sound?" — **Philosophical question***

*"If you build brilliant features and teachers won't assign them, do they even exist?" — **Philosophical question (adapted)***

In the last chapter, I showed you how EdTech's unique constraints—sales cycles, lock-in periods, seasonal access, and regulatory requirements— misalign with standard UX frameworks.

Let's dig deeper into the most confounding constraint: **the three-user dynamic.**

This is the EdTech reality that most frameworks completely ignore. UX approaches assume the person using your product is the person who chose it. Or that users can leave if they're unhappy. Or that you can optimize for "the user" as if there's only one type.

In EdTech? You have three completely different user types:

51

- **Administrators** who buy your product but rarely use it
- **Teachers** who control whether students ever see your product
- **Students** who use what they're assigned, whether they like it or not

And here's the kicker: Most EdTech companies spend the majority of their design effort on students (who have zero adoption control), the next largest on admins (who control purchasing but not usage), and the smallest on teachers (who control if your product ever actually makes it into student hands).

That mismatch? It creates the death spiral I've watched happen at company after company.

I would like to point out that not every EdTech product I've worked on had those *exact* user types. One was an educator evaluator tool—the users were admins (buying and using for compliance), evaluators, and evaluatees. Still three user types with three different sets of needs, goals, and frustrations. The design challenges all felt the same. I was just shifting from "teachers" to "evaluators" and from "students" to "evaluatees." The underlying dynamic remained the same: One group buys, another group controls the workflow, and a third group experiences the outcome with little say in the matter.

Your Brilliant Student Features Mean Nothing If Teachers Won't Use Them

You've built the most engaging student content in the world. Your AI-powered adaptive learning is brilliant. Your analytics dashboard would make a data scientist chef kiss. And none of it matters if your teacher interface is a nightmare.

I've lived this from both sides.

As a high school chemistry teacher for fifteen years, I quietly abandoned mandated programs that made my job harder, no matter how much the district paid for them or that I was "required" to use them.

As a UX professional, I've seen products with mediocre content thrive because the teacher experience was excellent. And I've watched products with exceptional content fail because the teacher interface added friction to already-overburdened educators.

Teachers are the gatekeepers to students.

If the teacher experience is cumbersome, confusing, or adds one more thing to an impossible workload, your product isn't going to get used. Period.

And if teachers don't use it, students never see that brilliant content you spent months perfecting.

Meet Your Three Users (Spoiler: They Want Different Things)

EdTech products serve three distinct user types with fundamentally different needs. Understanding who they are is step one. Understanding who controls what is step two.

Administrators: The Buyers Who Don't Use It

What they need: oversight, reporting, proof of ROI. They're making purchasing decisions, managing licenses, and justifying investments to superintendents or school boards.

How they use your product: quarterly, monthly, maybe weekly if they're very involved. They log in to check utilization dashboards, pull reports for board meetings, and make sure teachers are using what they paid for.

Their decision-making power: high for purchase and renewal. They control the budget. They make buying decisions based on features, compliance requirements, integration capabilities, and cost.

What they care about:

- Can this help us meet district goals?
- Can I prove to the board it's working?
- Does it integrate with our student information system?
- Will it survive an audit?

The critical insight: Admins buy based on promises. They renew based on proof.

Where things can go wrong: If your admin dashboards don't make it easy to demonstrate value, you lose renewals, even if teachers and students love the product.

Teachers: The Gatekeepers

What they need: efficiency, flexibility, and tools that fit their actual workflow. They're managing 30–150 students across multiple class sections or subjects, juggling learning objectives, accommodating different pacing needs, tracking progress, communicating with parents, and somehow also teaching.

How they use your product: multiple times daily. Before school to check who completed homework. During planning periods to set up assignments. During class to monitor student progress. After school to adjust upcoming lessons based on performance.

Their decision-making power: high control over whether students actually use your product, regardless of what admins purchased. Even "mandated" district tools get quietly abandoned when teachers find them unusable.

What they care about:

- Does this save me time or cost me time?
- Can I do this in four minutes between classes?
- Will this help my struggling students?
- Does this give me the data I need right now, not next week?
- Will I have to find meaning myself from raw data or endless tables?

The critical insight: Teachers are the rate-determining step (former chemistry teacher here—can't resist a good science analogy). They control whether students ever see your product, regardless of what features convinced admins to purchase or how brilliant your student content is. Admins make purchasing decisions, but teachers make adoption decisions.

Students: The End Users With No Say

What they need: engaging, intuitive learning experiences. They're your end users for learning outcomes—everything you're building should ultimately serve their learning.

How they use your product: daily, often multiple times per day. They need content that's appropriately challenging, interfaces that work on their (usually old) devices, and experiences that don't make them feel stupid when they struggle.

Their decision-making power: none. They use what the teacher assigns. In K–12 contexts, students are mandated to use district-adopted tools whether they like them or not.

What they care about:

- Is this going to take forever?
- Will I look dumb if I don't understand it?
- Does this work on my Chromebook?
- Can I do this at home, where the internet is spotty (or at school with its notoriously slow Wi-Fi)?

The critical insight: Student engagement matters, but only if teachers actually use your product.

Where things can go wrong: You can have the world's best student experience, but if assignment creation is cumbersome, teachers won't assign. If grading is time-consuming, teachers will use your product minimally. If workflow doesn't match how teachers actually work, students never see that brilliant content. And worse, as utilization goes down, it shows on those admin dashboards and reports, and they realize it's not worth the cost. Lost renewal.

The Death Spiral: What Happens When You Get the Teacher Interface Wrong

Let me walk you through what I've witnessed at multiple companies (and experienced as a teacher):

Stage 1: Optimistic Adoption

The district purchases your product. Admin sets it up. Teachers are told they'll be using it this semester. Everyone's hopeful because the product looked promising in the demo.

Stage 2: First Friction

A teacher logs in for the first time. It takes twenty minutes to figure out how to create their first assignment because the workflow assumes they already understand your internal product logic. You have just started losing them in this moment. They don't have twenty minutes. They're struggling to figure this out during their thirty-minute lunch break between teaching and supervising the cafeteria.

Stage 3: Daily Frustration

The teacher needs to differentiate an assignment for struggling students. Instead of adjusting parameters on the original, the interface requires creating entirely separate assignments. They spend forty-five minutes doing something that should take five. Now they're not just learning your system—they're fighting it. Every extra step convinces them the product doesn't understand how they actually work.

Stage 4: Critical Decision Point

The teacher wants to see which students completed last night's homework before class starts. The information exists, but it's buried three clicks deep in a dashboard designed for weekly analysis, not real-time classroom decisions. It's 7:45 a.m. and first period starts at 8:00. They give up and move on. This is where adoption actually dies, though you won't see it in your analytics. The teacher just decided your product adds more work than it removes.

Stage 5: Workaround Creation

The teacher has a brilliant lesson idea that would work perfectly with your content, but implementing it requires a workflow your interface doesn't support. They improvise a workaround that's so clunky they won't do it again. Your support team starts hearing "Well, what we do is ..." followed by convoluted multi-step processes. These workarounds are red flags that your workflow is broken

Stage 6: Quiet Abandonment

The teacher stops assigning work through your platform. They use it for district-mandated assessments only, the bare minimum to avoid getting called out by administrators. Even though the license shows "active," students rarely see your content.

Stage 7: District-Wide Impact

Admin sees terrible usage numbers across multiple teachers and questions whether to renew. Teachers complain to department chairs, who complain to principals. The product that looked so promising in the demo is now associated with frustration and wasted time.

The tragic irony? Your student experience really is excellent. But students never see it because the teacher experience adds friction instead of removing it.

The Teacher Context You Might Not Be Accounting For

If you want to understand why teacher interfaces fail, you need to understand what teachers are actually dealing with. Not in theory—in daily reality.

Real Example: Ideal Pedagogy vs. Classroom Reality

Personalized learning tools are fantastic for learning. As someone who ran my own classroom using mastery learning and personalized pathways, I wholeheartedly agree.

In reality, that's a really hard way to run a classroom. Many schools and districts aren't set up to allow teachers that type of radical flexibility. Common assessments given on specific dates, mandates about what to cover when, and district-wide pacing guides all work against it.

In all my years of teaching at various high schools, I worked with only a handful of teachers who were willing and able to make the shift to personalized learning. Later, I worked on a personalized learning product that gave students diagnostics and then presented each student with their own path to learn the content for their grade level. Fantastic in theory, but it struggled to gain real traction. Teachers consistently asked for features (like assigning specific skills to the entire class) that contradicted the product's underpinning philosophy: A new skill would be introduced to each student only when their personal progress indicated they were ready.

However, there's another approach that may still meet students where they are while recognizing the realities of the classroom. It doesn't require a teacher to handle each student working on something different and fits the district's scope and sequence, yet still presents students with the skills they need when they need them.

Instead of individualized paths, the product could allow teachers to indicate what unit they're working on in class and use the rich student progress data to suggest 3–4 small groups of students who need to work on the same supporting skills for the current unit. Teachers don't have to dig through data to see which skills students need and form groups themselves—the product does it for them based on its understanding of where students are and what learning progressions make sense for the teacher's unit goals. That way, the teacher has 3–4 small groups to manage instead of thirty individuals. Students still work on skills based on their needs, and everyone stays aligned with the current unit during whole-class instruction.

The fully individualized model is ideal for learning, but small groups working on shared skill needs fit classroom reality far better while still supporting whole class instruction.

So, which is better? A philosophically ideal product that doesn't get used, or one that understands the classroom context and still pushes toward a higher level of personalization in learning?

Time Poverty

Teachers don't have thirty minutes to "learn your system." They have four minutes between classes. They're planning lessons during lunch. They're grading at 10 p.m. after their own kids are in bed. (I was actually floored at the difference between teaching and corporate work once I made the shift. Even at its busiest, corporate life is nothing compared to teaching!) When your interface requires watching a fifteen-minute tutorial to do basic tasks, you've lost them.

Every extra step, every unclear button label, every "where did that option go?" moment costs them time they don't have. Your interface can't just be "usable"—it needs to be so intuitive that teachers can accomplish tasks without thinking about your interface at all.

Cognitive Load

Teachers are holding dozens of variables in their heads simultaneously:

- Which students need extra support with today's concept
- Whose parents they need to contact about missing work
- Which standards they're behind on for state tests
- When grades are due for the quarterly report
- Which students have 504 accommodations requiring modified assignments
- Who was absent yesterday and needs to make up the quiz
- Whether they can spend one more day on this unit or need to move on

Your interface can't add to that cognitive load—it needs to reduce it.

When your system requires teachers to remember what "asynchronous mode" means, or keep track of which template they used for which section, or recall the six-step process for creating differentiated assignments, you're adding cognitive work they don't have capacity for.

Your product needs to match their mental models and how they think about the work they do, not require them to understand your data structures and unique constraints.

Workflow Misalignment

Teachers don't think in terms of your product's data model. They think in terms of their actual tasks:

- "I need to assign homework differentiated by reading level."
- "I need to see who's struggling with fractions before tomorrow's lesson."
- "I need to prove to a parent that their child isn't turning in work."

When your interface is organized around your database schema instead of teachers' tasks, every interaction requires translation.

"I want to assign reading to my advanced students" becomes "First, I need to create a group, then filter by ... wait, is that in Student Management or Assignment Creation? Let me click around ..."

This translation work is exhausting. After doing it three times, teachers start looking for workarounds. After doing it ten times, they stop using features they actually need.

Multi-Section Reality

Most secondary teachers teach multiple sections of the same course—often with 3–6 sections of "eighth-grade Math" or "Biology."

Your interface needs to support this reality, not fight it.

What causes pain:

- Creating the same assignment five separate times (one per section)
- Grading 150 of the same assessment, one student at a time
- Adjusting pacing when Monday's lesson ran long, but having to adjust it manually for each of Tuesday's five sections
- Adjusting just one section's assignment without adjusting the others, because there was an assembly during that period
- Wanting to see performance across all algebra students, but your reports only work on one section at a time

What works:

- Create once, assign to multiple sections
- Bulk grading with the ability to add individual comments where needed
- Global pacing adjustments that propagate intelligently, but also don't *have* to be global.
- Aggregated views that respect how teachers think ("all my algebra classes" is a meaningful grouping)

Bulk operations aren't a "nice to have" for teachers—they're a lifesaver. Without them, your product takes five times longer than it should.

Real Classroom Constraints

Teachers can't always access your platform during class:

- The internet goes down (or is notoriously slow)
- Old Chromebooks take ten minutes to load your site
- They're teaching, not sitting at a computer
- School Wi-Fi blocks certain features
- Students' home internet is unreliable

If your product requires constant connectivity, real-time collaboration, or specific device capabilities, it will fail in many classroom contexts.

Teachers need to:

- Download critical materials for offline use
- Accomplish most common tasks on mobile or tablets (they're walking around the classroom, not chained to a desk)
- Work in low-bandwidth situations without the whole interface breaking

- Have a graceful fallback when technology inevitably fails

Education System Realities

Teachers operate within systems that constrain their choices. These realities vary by district, but they likely include some combination of:

Mandated curricula and pacing guides: Many districts require teachers to cover specific content on specific weeks. Your flexible, student-driven platform might work beautifully in theory, but if Mrs. Johnson has to teach fractions in week fourteen—the week of district benchmark assessments—your adaptive pacing feature becomes irrelevant.

Common assessments: When all eighth-grade math teachers give the same test on the same day, they need to be roughly aligned on pacing. Your product's ability to let students work at their own pace? Great for summer school or intervention, problematic for regular classroom use.

Administrative expectations: Teachers have administrators observing their classrooms, reviewing their lesson plans, and monitoring their grade distributions. If your product's approach doesn't align with what their principal expects to see, teachers won't use it—even if they believe in your philosophy.

State standards and testing pressures: Teachers are often evaluated based on student performance on state tests. If your product's scope and sequence don't align with their state's standards, or if the learning approach doesn't prepare students for the state test's format, teachers can't take the risk.

Technology access and policies: Some districts block certain websites or limit bandwidth. Some schools don't allow students to access technology at home. Some have one-to-one devices, others have shared carts of thirty laptops per 150 students. Your product needs to work within these constraints.

Professional development (PD) time: Teachers need time to learn new tools. If your product requires extensive training but the district only provides two hours of PD at the start of the year, adoption will suffer—not because teachers don't want to use it, but because they don't have time to learn it properly.

Philosophical alignment with school culture: Some schools emphasize direct instruction, others project-based learning. Some prioritize standardized test scores, others focus on social-emotional learning. If your product's underlying philosophy clashes with the school's culture, teachers face pressure to minimize its use.

The most successful EdTech products aren't the ones with the most research-backed pedagogy. They're the ones that meet teachers where they are—within the systems they actually operate in—while still moving the needle toward better learning outcomes.

Your product doesn't need to work in every classroom context. But it needs to work in the contexts where your target users actually teach. And that means understanding not just what teachers want to do, but what their systems allow them to do.

Design Attention vs. Adoption Control

Here's the pattern I see repeatedly:

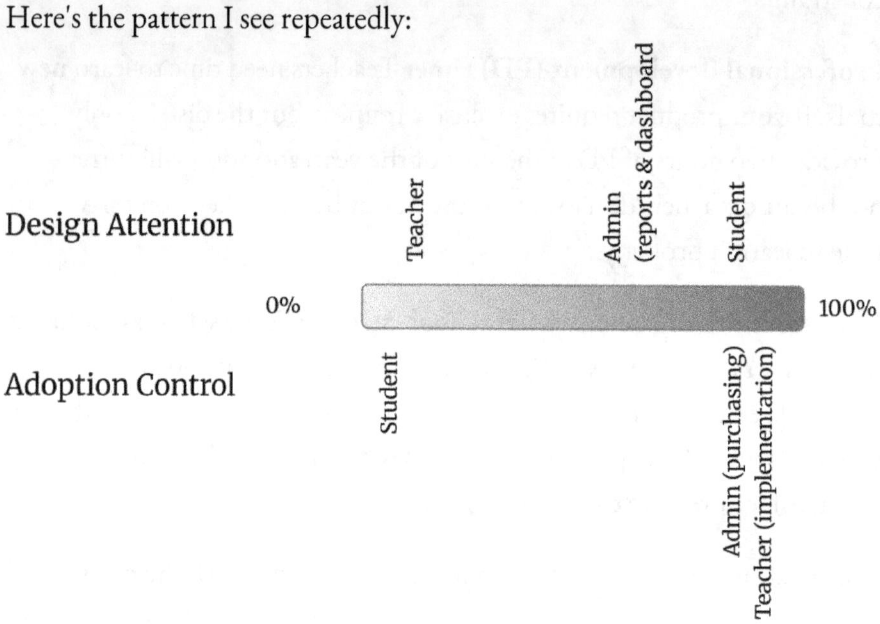

This mismatch creates the death spiral. You've optimized the wrong part of the system.

What "Alignment" Actually Means

When I talk about alignment, I'm not saying percentages need to match. Alignment means your design investment reflects the strategic importance of each user type to actual adoption and success, as well as the current state of your product.

Good alignment: Students have 10 percent adoption control but get 40 percent design attention because engaging student experience is your competitive differentiator—as long as you're also investing heavily in the teacher experience that enables access.

Poor alignment: Teachers have 80 percent adoption control but get 15 percent design attention because your team focuses on admin dashboards and student features, but you have a teacher NPS of 30.

The key question isn't "Do my percentages match?" It's "Am I investing design resources where they'll impact actual product adoption?"

The Questions Your Product Team Should Be Asking

Stop asking "What features do teachers need?" Start asking:

"What does a teacher's actual day look like?"

Not theoretically. Actually.

- When do they plan lessons? (Sunday evening, planning period, before school?)
- When do they grade? (During lunch, after school, at 10 p.m.?)
- When do they need data? (Before first period to see who did the homework? After class, to adjust tomorrow's lesson?)
- What device are they using? (Laptop at their desk? Tablet while walking around? Phone during passing period?)
- What other tools are they switching between? (Google Classroom, PowerSchool, email, their LMS ...)

When you understand their actual context, you'll design differently. You'll realize that a workflow requiring eight minutes of uninterrupted focus won't work during their four-minute passing period. You'll understand if mobile access isn't optional.

"What are the three things teachers do most often in our system?"

Get specific. For many EdTech products:

1. Create/assign work to students
2. Check who completed work and how they performed
3. Provide feedback or adjust upcoming lessons based on student performance

Now ask: Can teachers do those three things in under sixty seconds each? Without clicking through multiple screens? Without referencing documentation or needing training?

If not, those are your highest-priority UX improvements. Everything else can wait.

"How does our system fit into their existing workflow?"

Be honest:

- Are you *replacing* something they currently do, or *adding to* their workload?
- Do you integrate with their LMS, or are you yet another system to transfer information to/from?
- Can they accomplish tasks without switching contexts, or does using your product mean stopping everything else?

If you're adding work instead of reducing it, you need to provide disproportionate value to justify that addition. "Slightly better student analytics" won't cut it if teachers have to import data from three different systems to get a complete picture.

"What does 'assignment creation' actually involve for this teacher?"

Now you're getting beyond feature lists into actual workflow understanding.

Walk through it:

- Are they teaching one section or five sections of the same course?
- Do they differentiate by student or by section?
- Do they need to preview the student experience before publishing? (Spoiler alert: Yes!)
- What happens when they realize on Tuesday morning that Monday's lesson needs another day?
- Do they assign the same homework to everyone, or three different versions for different student groups?

When you understand the complete workflow, you'll design systems that support the whole task, not disconnected pieces that teachers have to manually stitch together.

"When a teacher opens our system at 6:45 a.m. before first period, what do they need to know immediately?"

Teachers don't open your product to explore. They open it with specific, urgent questions:

- Which students didn't do the homework? (I need to check in with them)
- Who's struggling with yesterday's concept? (I need to adjust today's lesson)
- What needs my attention before the bell rings in fifteen minutes? (I need to make sure today's lesson is "live" for students)

If your landing page shows generic dashboard metrics or requires teachers to navigate to different sections to answer these questions, you're wasting their most precious resource: the time right before class when they're trying to be responsive to student needs.

The home screen should surface immediately actionable information, not vanity metrics.

Red Flags That Your Teacher Interface Is Failing

Here are the warning signs I look for when auditing EdTech products:

Teachers are using workarounds

If your customer support team keeps hearing "Well, what we do is ..." followed by a convoluted multi-step process, your workflow is broken.

I've worked on a platform where teachers had to create duplicate classes in addition to the synced classes because they wanted to chunk content into units for students (and their gradebook), but the platform didn't allow that. Now they have duplicate classes—some synced, others they have to update manually if the roster changes—just to be able to organize content for students.

Common tasks require uncommon knowledge

If bulk assignment creation requires understanding "organization hierarchies" or "assignment templates," you've exposed your internal architecture in ways users shouldn't see. Your data model is for you. Teachers need to interact with your product using their mental model, not yours.

One product I worked on allowed teachers to create groups of students within the class, which most teachers use to differentiate for many reasons. They might want to select that subgroup and substitute one assignment for another, excuse an assignment, or add a supporting activity. However, the way the platform handled these groups was very different. It created an entirely separate list of assignments in addition to the class list of assignments. So a student had to choose either the whole class's assignment list or the subgroup's assignment list. Two separate lists, with no way to turn off the whole class list for that subgroup, and no way to merge the two to make sense for students. The platform handled the subgroup of students as if it were a completely separate class. The teachers had no reason to expect this behavior based on how subgroups actually work in the classrooms, and the mismatch caused significant frustration for both teachers and students.

Teachers can't figure out your system without training

Some training is fine for advanced features. But if teachers can't do basic tasks intuitively on day one, you've failed.

I've seen EdTech companies create multi-page quick-start guides and fifteen-minute tutorial videos for "creating your first assignment." That's not a sign of feature richness—it's a sign that your interface is confusing.

Teachers will use products that they can learn in five minutes by exploring. They'll abandon products that require certification courses to use effectively, no matter how powerful.

Your interface requires teachers to make decisions without adequate context

If you're asking teachers to choose between "synchronous" and "asynchronous" modes before explaining what that means for their students, you've put your product model ahead of user understanding. Every decision point in your interface adds cognitive load. If teachers don't have the information they need to make that decision confidently, they'll either choose randomly (leads to mistakes), abandon the task (kills adoption), or resort to Google for help (costs time they don't have).

And they'll *really* be frustrated if they can't change that decision later on, once they do fully understand the implications or have had time to see it in action.

Critical information requires hunting

If a teacher has to click through three screens to answer "Did Sarah complete yesterday's assignment?" your information architecture is wrong. Common information should be immediately accessible. Teachers shouldn't need to remember navigation paths or search through nested menus to answer the questions they ask every single day. Better yet, let teachers customize how their homescreen looks with the information they access most frequently!

Your system fights how teachers actually work

If they're teaching five sections of the same course but have to do everything five separate times, your design doesn't match reality. If they can't easily adjust pacing when a lesson runs long, your rigid structure will frustrate them daily.

Teachers work in patterns. Their daily, weekly, and yearly rhythms are predictable. Your product should support those natural patterns, not force teachers to adapt to your system's arbitrary constraints.

Why This Matters for Your Business

This isn't just about user experience—it's about business survival.

Teacher churn is expensive. Every teacher who stops using your product represents dozens or hundreds of students who won't engage with your content. When teachers complain to admins, admins question renewals. When usage numbers tank, you lose accounts.

But when teachers love your interface—when it actually saves them time, reduces their stress, and helps them teach better—they become your best salespeople. They tell other teachers. They request that their department adopt your product. They push back when admins suggest switching to competitors.

Word of mouth among teachers is powerful. One enthusiastic teacher advocate is worth more than any marketing budget, because teachers trust other teachers more than they trust vendor promises.

Conversely, one frustrated teacher can torpedo adoption across an entire school. "Don't bother with Product X, it's terrible" spreads fast in teacher lounges and Facebook groups.

The Hill I'll Die On

If you have to choose between improving your student-facing features or your teacher interface, improve the teacher interface every time—at least until the teacher experience is genuinely solid.

Not because the student experience doesn't matter—it absolutely does. But because the teacher is the gatekeeper to the student experience. A slightly less polished student interface that teachers actually use will drive better learning outcomes than the world's most innovative student features that sit unused because teachers can't efficiently assign them.

I've fought for this prioritization repeatedly. When product roadmap debates centered on "Should we build this cool new student feature or fix this teacher workflow frustration?" I advocated for the teacher workflow every single time. Because I know what happens when you get the teacher experience wrong. I've lived it as a teacher, forced to use mandated tools that made my job harder. And I've seen it as a UX strategist, watching brilliant EdTech products fail because they neglected the gatekeepers.

This is especially critical in K–12, where teachers control adoption completely. Even if a district "mandates" that teachers use a program, that doesn't mean they actually do it effectively. **Teachers are masters of malicious compliance—they'll use your product just enough to avoid getting in trouble, but not enough to generate any value.** (Yeah, I did it … and I'd do it again!)

Moving Forward

You now understand the three-user dynamic—buyers (admins), gatekeepers (teachers), and end users (students) each have different needs and control. Teachers are the rate-determining step, so designing disproportionately for users who don't control adoption guarantees failure.

Next, we'll shift from problems to principles. You'll learn the six core principles EdTech companies actually need: confidence thresholds over perfect research, fast-to-insight over comprehensive studies, outcomes over features, context-driven method selection, stakeholder buy-in throughout, and showing users rather than quoting them.

75

CHAPTER 4

The Principles Behind Strategic Tool Selection

*"It's not about having time. It's about making time." — **Unknown***

*"'And in EdTech, it's about making time before August." —**Unknown** (adapted)*

From Pre-Built Frameworks to Building Your Own Toolkit

Think about building a toolkit for home repairs. You don't buy someone else's pre-assembled toolbox and force yourself to use only those tools regardless of your projects.

You assess what kind of work you do most often. You choose tools that fit your specific needs. You add specialized tools as you encounter new challenges. You adapt techniques based on what works in your situation.

That's what this book teaches you to do with UX methods in EdTech.

The tools themselves—user interviews, usability testing, journey mapping, opportunity mapping, task analysis, prototyping—those exist across various frameworks. You're not inventing new tools.

You're learning:

- Which tools fit *your* constraints
- How to select tools that get you to confident decisions the fastest
- How to adapt tools when standard approaches don't fit
- How to use tools effectively in EdTech's unique context

Your toolkit is the collection of methods you've chosen and adapted for your specific EdTech situation.

It's strategic because it fits your reality. It's practical because you built it from understanding your constraints, not from following someone else's prescription.

The Tools Come From Everywhere

Here's what makes this approach powerful: You're not rejecting Design Thinking, Continuous Discovery, or JTBD. You're learning when to use their tools and when to adapt them.

From Design Thinking: Empathy-building observations, rapid prototyping, collaborative synthesis. Use when you have flexible timelines and workshop capacity.

From Continuous Discovery: Weekly touchpoints with users, opportunity mapping, assumption testing. Use when you have continuous user access and responsive roadmaps.

From JTBD: Task-based design thinking, forces analysis, and struggling moments. Use when you're researching specific workflows and decision points.

Custom approaches: Methods you design when standard tools don't fit your constraints.

The strategic shift: You're not choosing a framework. You're choosing tools from any source based on what your context demands.

The Six Principles: Your Guide for Building Your Toolkit

The six principles in this chapter aren't another framework to follow. They're your decision-making guide for toolkit-building:

Principle 1 (Confidence Thresholds): Helps you determine which tools you need for this specific decision (because not all decisions are created equal).

Principle 2 (Fast-to-Insight): Guides you toward tools that respect EdTech's time constraints.

Principle 3 (Outcomes Over Features): Shows you which tools reveal what users actually need.

Principle 4 (Context-Driven Selection): Teaches you how to assess which tools fit your reality.

Principle 5 (Stakeholder Buy-In): Directs you toward tools that build ownership.

Principle 6 (Show Users): Identifies the tool that makes problems undeniable.

Think of these principles as your selection criteria—the questions you ask before choosing which tools to put in your toolbox.

Principle 1: Confidence Thresholds Over Perfect Research

Here's a truth that changes everything about how you approach research: **Not every decision requires the same level of confidence.** Choosing a button color? Being 60 percent confident is fine. Ship it, see what happens, adjust if needed. Redesigning your entire onboarding flow right before school starts? You need 85–90 percent confidence before committing. Rebuilding your platform architecture? You should be 95 percent-plus confident, because this is a multi-year bet-the-company decision.

Confidence threshold thinking asks: "How confident should we be to move forward with this decision?"

Once you know that, you can work backward to the minimum research needed to hit that confidence level.

What Creates Confidence?

Confidence doesn't come from following a research checklist. It comes from triangulation:

- **Multiple signals:** Qualitative interviews confirmed by quantitative data

- **Diverse stakeholders:** All three user types represented (admins, teachers, students) as appropriate for the decision
- **Strategic alignment:** User needs + business goals + technical feasibility all point in the same direction
- **Validation through testing:** Not just theorizing. You've watched users actually accomplish tasks with your solution

The Confidence Spectrum

Different decisions carry different risks:

Quick wins / minor improvements: 60–70 percent confident

- Risk is low, and decisions are fairly easily reversible.
- Don't over-research low-stakes decisions.

Medium features / workflow changes: 80 percent confident

- Risk is moderate, some reversibility, but not painless.
- Balance rigor with timeline constraints.

Platform changes / major releases: 90 percent+ confident

- Risk is high, very difficult to reverse
- Worth the time investment to get it right

The strategic insight: Having 60 percent confidence is sufficient for some decisions. Don't spend weeks researching what you could test in production with minimal risk.

And conversely: Don't ship major changes with only 60 percent confidence when users are locked in for nine months and can't leave if you got it wrong.

Part 2 shows you how to determine which confidence level you need and the fastest path to reach it, given your specific EdTech constraints.

Principle 2: Fast-to-Insight Over Comprehensive Research

The best research process isn't the most thorough one. **It's the one that gets you to confident decisions fastest.** This doesn't mean cutting corners or rushing research. It means being strategic about:

- **Strategic sampling over volume:** Five well-selected participants often reveal patterns as clearly as thirty random ones.
- **Parallel streams over sequential:** While waiting for IRB approval, run analytics and admin interviews simultaneously.
- **Rolling synthesis over batch analysis:** Debrief after each session. Patterns are visible by interview five, instead of waiting until after interview twenty.
- **Focused questions over broad exploration:** When the timeline is tight, know what you need to learn and go straight there.

The Ph.D. Researcher's Dilemma

I have a bachelor's in chemistry and a Ph.D. in innovative instructional design. I was trained in rigorous experimental design, statistical analysis, and systematic research protocols. And I've learned that academic rigor—while valuable—moves too slowly for product decisions. In academia, you can spend six months on a study because publication timelines allow it. In EdTech, six months means missing the adoption window for another year.

The strategic shift: Apply the *thinking* of rigorous research (clear hypotheses, triangulated evidence, validated conclusions) without the *timelines* of academic research (comprehensive literature reviews, massive sample sizes, multiple experimental conditions).

When Fast-to-Insight Matters Most

At one company, we had ten months to research, design, build, and launch a complete platform rebuild with an immovable August deadline and no budget for research incentives or usability testing. That meant research couldn't consume six months—we'd miss the only launch window that mattered, and it had to be free from cash costs. We used every existing research source (sales calls, support tickets, prior observations) and did usability testing on volunteers from throughout the organization (not ideal, but better than nothing!).

The result was an 18 percent increase in student rostering completion and a 41 percent increase in diagnostic completion. We launched on time with strong adoption from day one.

We would have failed had we tried to do comprehensive research with weekly teacher interviews. Teachers weren't available during the school year, and sequential research would have blown our timeline entirely.

The principle: Strategic speed comes from smart scoping and parallel work.

Part 2 shows you the specific techniques—strategic sampling, rolling synthesis, parallel research streams—that make fast-to-insight possible without sacrificing confidence.

Principle 3: Outcomes Over Features

When stakeholders or users tell you they want a feature, they're usually describing a solution for a problem they're experiencing.

Your job isn't to build the feature they want. Your job is to understand the outcome they need to achieve and design the workflow that enables it.

Translating Feature Requests

- **When someone says**: "We need bulk grading."

They actually mean: "I need to give feedback on 150 assignments in under two hours—not spend my entire weekend grading."

Design for: the complete workflow of assignment review, feedback provision, and progress tracking—not just a "bulk" button.

- **When someone says**: "We need better search."

They actually mean: "I can't find the assignment I created last week, and I'm four minutes away from class starting."

Design for: quick access to recently used items, predictable organization, and context-aware defaults. Search might not even be the right solution.

- **When someone says:** "We need an AI tutor."

They actually mean: "My struggling students need help when I can't get to them individually, and I need to know that it's actually helping."

Design for: the ecosystem of student support, teacher oversight, and progress visibility. AI might be part of it, but the outcome is "struggling students get unstuck," not "there's an AI feature."

Task-Based Design Thinking

In EdTech products, this shift from features to outcomes means:

Instead of: Search feature, filter feature, export feature, bulk actions feature—all scattered across the interface.

Design for: "Assign licenses before school starts" as a complete workflow with all capabilities in logical sequence.

Instead of: Grading tools, feedback tools, progress tracking, parent communication—in different parts of your product.

Design for: "Give meaningful feedback on student work" as an integrated workflow.

Instead of: Content library, assignment creator, progress monitoring, reporting—separate features.

Design for: "Differentiate instruction for struggling students" as a supported task flow.

Three Questions for Every Feature Request

- **What outcome does the user need to achieve?** Not what feature do they want, but what goal are they trying to accomplish?
- **What's the complete workflow from trigger to goal?** Map the entire task, not just the moment they'd use this feature.
- **Where do all three user types fit into this workflow?** In EdTech, there's almost always a chain: Teacher assigns → Student completes → Admin reviews reports.

Part 2 (Chapter 9) shows you how to map complete workflows, design for outcomes rather than features, and handle the complexity when all three user types interact with the same workflow.

Principle 4: Context-Driven Method Selection

Here's where everything from Chapters 1–3 comes together into a practical approach.

The question isn't "Which framework should I use?" but "Given my specific context and constraints, which tools will get me to confident decisions fastest?"

Part 2 walks you through assessing each dimension systematically (Chapter 6), then shows you how to translate that context into strategic method selection (Chapter 7).

Principle 5: Building Stakeholder Buy-In Throughout

This is where many research efforts stumble, even when the research itself is excellent.

Research doesn't drive decisions by being brilliant. Research drives decisions when stakeholders feel ownership of the findings.

I learned this the hard way.

Early on, I'd conduct research, synthesize findings, and present polished recommendations to stakeholders. The presentations went well. Everyone nodded. Then, in the days and weeks that followed, everyone questioned everything, and no one was ready to act on the insights.

The problem wasn't the research quality. The problem was that stakeholders experienced research as something I *reported to them* rather than something we *discovered together*.

When I changed my approach—involving stakeholders throughout the process rather than just at the end—everything shifted.

The Fundamental Insight

Research that drives decisions isn't research that's comprehensive or methodologically perfect. It's research that stakeholders participated in creating. When product managers help shape research questions before you start, they're committed to acting on answers. When engineers see emerging themes weekly during research, they're not surprised by final recommendations. And when stakeholders participate in synthesis—watching clips together, identifying patterns as a group—they feel they discovered the insights, not that you're reporting your conclusions.

By the time you formally present, stakeholders already own the findings because they helped generate them.

Why This Matters More in EdTech

Remember from Chapters 1–3: EdTech has immovable deadlines, lock-in periods, and seasonal access windows that standard frameworks ignore. You don't have time for research that generates perfect insights no one acts on. You can't afford to spend months researching only to have stakeholders dismiss findings they're hearing for the first time.

Strategic stakeholder involvement isn't just good practice—it's survival in constrained EdTech environments.

Part 2 (Chapter 8) shows you exactly how to involve stakeholders throughout research execution—before, during, and after—so findings drive decisions instead of sitting ignored.

Principle 6: Show Users, Don't Just Quote Them

One of the most powerful tools for building stakeholder buy-in? **Showing clips of actual users.** Not just quotes. Not just paraphrasing what users said. Actual video or audio clips of real people struggling, succeeding, or reacting.

Why Clips Work When Quotes Don't

Clips can't be dismissed. When a stakeholder watches a teacher, someone who's taught for fifteen years, spend eight minutes trying to figure out how to differentiate an assignment and finally give up in frustration? That lands differently.

Clips build empathy. Reading about frustration is abstract. Watching someone struggle creates an emotional connection.

Clips are memorable. Months later, stakeholders will reference "that teacher who couldn't find her assignment" or "the admin who got lost in the license flow."

Clips create urgency. Watching users fail makes the problem feel immediate and real, not theoretical.

When Clips Change Everything

At one company, I showed a ninety-second clip of an administrator trying to assign licenses. She clicked through multiple screens, backtracked twice, and finally said out loud, "I have no idea if that worked." That clip did more to drive prioritization than any synthesis deck could have.

Clips don't just support your insights—they make stakeholders *feel* the problem. And when stakeholders feel the problem, they're motivated to solve it.

Part 2 (Chapter 8) shows you how to use clips strategically: when to pull them during synthesis, how to match them to stakeholder concerns, and how to integrate them into presentations and roadmap discussions so they drive action.

Building Your Toolkit: What Comes Next

The six principles you've just learned aren't abstract theory. They're practical guides for the toolkit you'll build in Part 2.

From Principles to Your Toolkit

Principle 1 (Confidence Thresholds) guides **Phase 1** (Assess Context) and **Phase 2** (Select Tools):

- You'll assess what's at stake in your specific situation.
- You'll determine how confident you need to be.
- You'll select tools that reach that confidence level fastest.

Principle 2 (Fast-to-Insight) guides **Phase 3** (Execute Research):

- You'll learn strategic sampling techniques.
- You'll apply rolling synthesis approaches.
- You'll run parallel research streams when access is limited.

Principle 3 (Outcomes Over Features) guides **Phase 4** (Develop Strategy) and **Phase 5** (Design Solutions):

- You'll translate feature requests into outcome needs.
- You'll map complete workflows, not disconnected features.
- You'll design for task completion, not feature usage.

Principle 4 (Context-Driven Selection) guides **all five phases**:

- You'll assess your organizational maturity and EdTech constraints.

- You'll select methods that fit your reality.
- You'll adapt tools when standard approaches don't work.

Principle 5 (Stakeholder Buy-In) guides **Phase 3** (Execute Research) and **Phases 4-5** (Advocate):

- You'll involve stakeholders throughout the research.
- You'll build ownership before presenting recommendations.
- You'll advocate effectively for both direction and solutions.

Principle 6 (Show Users) guides **Phase 3** (Execute Research) and **Phases 4-5** (Advocate):

- You'll pull strategic clips during research.
- You'll use clips to build empathy with stakeholders.
- You'll reference clips in roadmap discussions months later.

These aren't separate ideas—they're integrated strategic thinking.

The principles provide the "why" behind your toolkit. Part 2 provides the "how" for building it.

That's not a framework. That's a toolkit you built.

CHAPTER 5

How the Toolkit Comes Together

"Give a man a fish, and you feed him for a day. Teach a man to fish, and you feed him for a lifetime." — **Chinese proverb**

"Give a team a framework, and they work for a sprint. Teach them to build a toolkit, and they solve problems forever." — **Chinese proverb (adapted)**

You now understand why standard frameworks have issues in EdTech. You've seen the possible constraints. You've watched six framework misalignments waste research effort. You know the six principles for building your own toolkit.

Part 2 shows you how to build it.

What Experience Taught Me About Frameworks

I've worked at multiple EdTech companies as a founding designer. Each time, I walked into a different reality. And that reality continued to evolve the entire time I was there. No single framework could have worked across all of them—each reality demanded a different set of tools.

Here are three scenarios I've encountered firsthand:

Scenario #1: Proving UX Value Before You Can Practice It

At a state education agency, I inherited an educator evaluator tool meant to help school districts comply with state legislation. The department had non-existent UX maturity, zero research budget, and was not even aware that anything was wrong with their tool. They hired me as a program consultant, not a UX professional. Yet I had to provide convincing proof that UX was worth investing in before I could even talk about comprehensive research—and before the ultimately hugely successful rebuild.

Scenario #2: When the Timeline Won't Wait for Perfect Process

Before I arrived on the scene of a non-profit, they'd had some dispersed ad hoc UX work. I had leadership support for building a UX function from scratch. But we faced an extremely aggressive timeline for bringing the product in-house to regain control: ten months to research, design, build, and launch a complete platform rebuild. The timeline dictated everything.

Scenario #3: Rebuilding Trust While Rebuilding the Product

At another company, I walked into a recent restructuring and distrust of how user research and product management had been done previously. We had to prove to our sales and support teams that we were going to make real changes for users, and that we would deliver on the promises we were making. We also had to convince the engineering department that changes needed to be made—no, our product didn't "already do the thing customers were needing it to do"—and that we could deliver by the deadline. All with a six-month lead time while the product managers and I were being onboarded to the new product department. The research had to be fast, wide-reaching, and accurate. And it had to be actionable in a way that not only improved usability, but also combatted two decades of organizational inertia and an attitude of "this is how we've always done it."

Lessons Learned

Each scenario presented completely different timing, access, regulatory, technical, and organizational constraints (see Chapter 1). Applying the same framework to all three would have been strategic malpractice. None of those efforts succeeded because we followed a framework with high fidelity. They succeeded because we understood the context deeply enough to know which tools to use when.

Let me show you what the constraints and solutions look like in practice.

Scenario #2: When the Timeline Won't Wait for Perfect Process

Our advantage: Access to users and leadership buy-in for UX

Constraints:

- Timing: ten months away from the next back-to-school launch
- Technical: a third-party platform that we'd outgrown and had little control over
- Organizational: no budget for research or testing

Our approach:

- Deep digging for all the existing data we could find (using existing research tools)
- Taking the risk of rebuilding the entire platform in-house to get out from under the constraints imposed by the third-party platform and engineering
- Iterative validation and ruthless editing during the ten-month build
- Pre-launch testing with existing users (those who start school earlier than most)

<u>Scenario #3: Rebuilding Trust While Rebuilding the Product</u>

Our advantage: A research budget and access to users

Constraints

- Timing: six months before the back-to-school release
- Technical debt: a 25-year-old sprawling product
- Regulatory: noncompliant WCAG platform
- Organizational: significant internal mistrust in the new product team's ability
- Organizational: inertia due to fixed processes

Our approach

- Strategic sampling (eight interviews, not fifteen) to reach 80 percent confidence in three weeks (fast validation tools)
- Focus on rebuilding the user experience (admin center) that was already slated for updating due to a decades-old platform that wasn't WCAG-compliant.

- Wait for the more complicated rebuild (teacher center) when we would have a full school year cycle to research, test, and build (triangulating product, tech debt, and business needs)
- Iterative usability testing via an unmoderated testing platform that found users for us based on our demographic requests to truncate the validation and iteration time before the rapid build process (larger pool and faster access/turnaround instead of recruiting current users)

Both approaches were strategic. Both used the same underlying principles from Chapter 4. But the toolkits I built for each situation looked nothing alike—which is exactly the point.

The Five-Phase Toolkit-Building Process

Before you think "here's another linear process," let me be clear: The five phases I'm about to lay out for toolkit-building aren't steps you complete sequentially and never revisit. They're the thinking process behind choosing which tools belong in *your* toolkit, and you'll adapt them as your context changes.

Here's an overview of each phase.

Phase 1: Assess Context (Chapter 6)

Question: What's actually true about our situation?

What you're doing: Understanding two layers of your context—organizational (UX maturity, roadmap flexibility, technical debt) and EdTech-specific (sales cycles, three-user dynamics, lock-in periods, access barriers, political landscape).

Purpose: Know your reality before choosing your tools. The same problem in different contexts requires different tools.

What this adds to your toolkit: This equips you with context awareness that guides every subsequent tool choice.

Phase 2: Select Tools and Artifacts (Chapter 7)

Question: Given our situation, which tools get us to confident decisions fastest?

What you're doing: Choosing research methods (user interviews, usability testing, analytics, etc.) that match your confidence thresholds, selecting communication artifacts (user flows, journey maps, prototypes) based on stakeholders and goals, and deciding between fast validation tools and deep discovery tools.

Purpose: Context-driven tool selection, not "best practices" application.

Strategic decision: How confident must we be? What's the fastest path to that confidence given our timeline, access, and risk level?

What this adds to your toolkit: You'll have the actual methods you'll use—chosen strategically, not prescribed by a framework.

Phase 3: Execute Research and Build Buy-In (Chapter 8)

Question: How do we use our selected tools effectively to drive decisions?

What you're doing: Fast but rigorous execution (strategic sampling, rolling synthesis, parallel work), progressive stakeholder involvement (not surprise presentations), strategic use of clips to build empathy.

Purpose: Research that drives decisions, not just generates insights.

What this adds to your toolkit: You'll have execution strategies for using your tools to effectively navigate EdTech's unique constraints.

Phase 4: Develop Strategy and Advocate for Direction (Chapter 9)

Question: What did we learn, what strategy should guide us, and which problems should we pursue?

What you're doing: Interpreting research findings strategically, developing your UX Strategy as a decision filter, advocating for which problems and opportunities to pursue, and building stakeholder alignment on strategic direction.

Purpose: Synthesize insights into strategic direction before investing in detailed design work.

Why this matters: Getting directional buy-in first means you design solutions that stakeholders are already committed to pursuing.

What this adds to your toolkit: You'll have strategic synthesis and advocacy tools for turning insights into organizational commitment.

Phase 5: Design Solutions and Advocate for Prioritization (Chapter 10)

Question: How do we translate strategy into designed solutions and get them prioritized and shipped?

What you're doing: Designing complete workflows that enable outcomes (not disconnected features), creating artifacts to communicate and validate design (user flows, storyboards, prototypes), advocating for designed solutions to be prioritized on the roadmap, compromising strategically when necessary, and measuring impact.

Purpose: Turn strategic direction into shipped product improvements that users actually experience.

Why advocacy matters: Brilliant design recommendations that sit unused don't help anyone.

What this adds to your toolkit: You'll be equipped with design and implementation advocacy tools for getting solutions built and shipped.

How These Phases Build Your Toolkit

The phases aren't linear—they inform each other continuously as you build and refine your toolkit.

Context assessment (Phase 1) is the lens to help determine which tools fit (Phase 2). But sometimes selecting tools reveals context you didn't initially see, sending you back to reassess. Or your context simply changes— leadership shifts, regulatory updates, resource allocation adjustments, board direction pivots—and you need to reassess which tools still fit.

Stakeholder involvement during research (Phase 3) often surfaces new constraints that affect your strategy (Phase 4) and designed solutions (Phase 5). Those constraints might require going back to Phase 2 to select different tools.

Strategic direction from Phase 4 guides which design tools you need in Phase 5. But sometimes designing solutions reveals that your strategy needs refinement—or that you need different tools to validate the design.

Design advocacy (Phase 5) builds organizational credibility that increases UX maturity, changing your context for the next cycle, and determining which tools will work.

Think of these as the toolkit-building process, not steps you check off.

How the Five Phases Operationalize the Six Principles

Remember the six principles from Chapter 4? Here's how they guide your toolkit-building through these five phases.

Principle 1: Confidence Thresholds Over Perfect Research

Operationalized in: Phases 1 and 2

Phase 1 context assessment reveals what's at stake—the decision's risk level determines the confidence you need. Phase 2 tool selection matches research tools to reach that confidence efficiently.

The tactical question "How many interviews should we do?" becomes the strategic question "How confident must we be to act, and which tools get us there fastest?"

Principle 2: Fast-to-Insight Over Comprehensive Research

Operationalized in: Phase 3

Phase 3 execution shows you the specific techniques for speed: strategic sampling, rolling synthesis, and parallel research streams. The principle becomes practice in how you use your selected tools.

Principle 3: Outcomes Over Features

Operationalized in: Phases 4 and 5

Phase 4 strategy development translates feature requests into outcome-focused opportunities. Phase 5 design uses tools that build workflows enabling those outcomes rather than disconnected features.

When users say "we need bulk grading," Phases 4 and 5 show you which tools help you dig for the actual outcome, giving meaningful feedback efficiently without adding time to their day.

Principle 4: Context-Driven Method Selection

Operationalized in: Phases 1 and 2

Phase 1 assesses your context across two layers—organizational constraints like maturity, roadmap flexibility, technical debt, and EdTech constraints like sales cycles and three-user dynamics. Phase 2 translates that context assessment into strategic tool choices that fit your reality.

Principle 5: Building Stakeholder Buy-In Throughout

Operationalized in: Phases 3, 4, and 5

Phase 3 shows you how to involve stakeholders progressively during research—before it begins, during execution, in mid-research synthesis, and through pre-presentation previews.

Phase 4 shows you how to get buy-in on strategic direction before investing in detailed design.

Phase 5 shows you how to advocate for designed solutions to be prioritized.

Throughout all three, findings drive decisions instead of sitting ignored in documents and reports.

Principle 6: Show Users, Don't Just Quote Them

Operationalized in: Phases 3, 4, and 5

Phase 3 provides the strategic approach to using clips during research—when to pull them, how to use them in presentations, and how to match them to stakeholder concerns.

Phase 4 shows how to use clips when advocating for strategic direction and problems to pursue.

Phase 5 shows how clips become lasting reference points in roadmap discussions and executive reviews, making abstract priorities concrete.

What Your Toolkit Is and Isn't

Before we dive into Phase 1, let me be clear about what you're building and what you're not.

Your toolkit IS:

- **A strategic collection of tools** (research methods, design approaches, advocacy techniques) you've selected based on your specific EdTech constraints, organizational maturity, and decision needs.
- **Adaptable to your situation.** Your maturity level, your timeline, and your constraints determine which tools you choose.
- **Built from methods that exist across frameworks**. You're not inventing new tools, you're learning which existing tools to select when.
- **Integrated across research, strategy, design, and advocacy.** Because UX isn't just research and screen designs, it's developing strategic direction, translating insights into designed solutions, and building the case for why they should be prioritized.

Your toolkit IS NOT:

- **Another prescriptive framework with specific tools you must use**. You're learning strategic thinking about tool selection, not following a checklist.
- **Complete from day one.** You build your toolkit iteratively based on what your context demands. Different projects may require different tools.
- **One-size-fits-all**. Your context determines which tools you select. I'll show you how to assess context and think strategically about tool selection—I won't prescribe exactly which tools to use in every situation.
- **A replacement for your judgment**. This toolkit-building process teaches you to make informed decisions about which tools to select—it doesn't make decisions for you.

For tactical implementation details:

If you want step-by-step guides for using specific tools—how to conduct interviews, create user flows, run usability tests, build business cases— that's what *The Strategic UX Toolkit Playbook* provides.

Think of this book as teaching you which tools to select and when. The Playbook teaches you how to use those tools effectively.

If you want to try specific tools before committing to the full approach, check out the free resources at kellymorganux.com: the Strategic User Interview Guide, and the Context Mapping Workbook.

Strategic Compromise and Knowing When to Fight

Before we move on, I want to talk about a skill that complements every toolkit you build: strategic compromise. Never leave home without it. Knowing when to compromise and when to hold firm can make the difference between whether you get to deploy your toolkit—or not.

Perfect advocacy doesn't mean getting everything you ask for. Strategic advocacy means knowing which battles to fight, where to compromise, and how to trade for what matters most.

Not Every Hill Is Worth Dying On

You'll face situations where stakeholders push back on your recommendations:

"We don't have time to test that thoroughly."

"Engineering says it's too complex."

"That's not how we've done things before."

"The business needs feature X more than users need what you're proposing."

Some push-back is legitimate. Some is solvable. Some require strategic compromise.

The strategic question: "Is this compromise acceptable, or does it undermine the core user value?"

Identify Your Non-Negotiables

Before entering advocacy discussions, know what you can't compromise on.

These are usually:

- **Core workflow integrity:** If the compromise breaks the task flow, users can't succeed.
- **Accessibility requirements:** If the compromise makes the product unusable for some users, it's not negotiable.
- **Data quality/security:** If the compromise creates data risks, it threatens both users and the business.
- **Fundamental UX strategy:** If the compromise contradicts your validated strategy, it undermines your strategic direction.

When to Stand Firm

Sometimes you need to push back hard—when compromises would:

<u>Violate accessibility requirements:</u>

"I understand development is complex, but we can't ship without keyboard navigation. We'll fail accessibility audits and exclude users who need assistive technology. This isn't negotiable."

<u>Break core workflows:</u>

"Removing draft state saving means users lose work if they get interrupted, which happens constantly in classrooms. They'll stop using the feature entirely. We need to solve this before launch."

<u>Contradict validated UX strategy:</u>

"This approach contradicts our strategy of acting as an instructional coach. Users validated that strategy because it matches how they want to work. Reverting to a feature dump undermines our strategic direction."

<u>Create technical debt that blocks future improvement:</u>

"This quick fix creates architectural constraints that prevent the improvements that we validated users need. We'll have to rebuild it completely in six months. Let's do it right now."

<u>Error prevention:</u>

"We can simplify the workflow by removing error prevention. Just show error messages after submission."

This violates task-based design principles and your UX strategy of filling knowledge gaps. The compromise would create user frustration and support burden. Not negotiable.

> **Strategic principle:** Strategic compromise isn't about giving in—it's about trading what's negotiable to protect what isn't.

Identify Where You Can Compromise

Many design details are negotiable if they preserve core user value:

Visual polish vs. functional workflow:

If stakeholders need to ship faster, you can launch with less visual polish if the workflow is solid. Polish can be added post-launch. Fixing broken workflows can't wait without frustrating users, even though you're fixing things.

Comprehensive features vs. focused MVP:

If the scope is too large, identify the minimum workflow that provides value. "We can ship license assignment without bulk operations in v1, add bulk in v2" might be acceptable if individual assignment still works well.

Perfect solution vs. good-enough improvement:

If the perfect solution requires rebuilding platform architecture, maybe a good-enough solution that works within current constraints is acceptable—if it genuinely improves user experience and doesn't create technical debt that blocks future improvement.

<u>Strategic trade-offs:</u>

"If we can't get designer time for three months, let's prioritize the admin workflow that threatens renewals over the teacher feature that's nice-to-have."

How to Propose Compromises Strategically

When you need to compromise, propose trade-offs that preserve core value:

<u>If we can't do X, can we do Y instead?</u>

"If we can't test with fifteen teachers, can we test with five strategically selected teachers who represent our key segments? That gets us to 80 percent confidence instead of 95 percent, which is acceptable for this decision."

<u>If we must cut scope, let's cut feature Z but keep workflow integrity</u>

"If the development timeline is locked, we can launch without the bulk assignment feature, but we need to keep error prevention and progress visibility—those are what make individual assignment successful."

<u>If we ship it imperfect now, what's the commitment to improve later?</u>

"If we ship with known usability issues because the timeline is critical, let's commit that the next sprint addresses those issues before we add new features. We can't leave users with a broken workflow indefinitely."

Building Capital for Battles That Matter

You can't fight every battle. Strategic advocacy means building capital so you have credibility when battles really matter.

Pick your battles:

- Fight hard for non-negotiables.
- Compromise strategically on negotiables.
- Let go of things that don't matter to users.

Show results:

- When your recommendations succeed, publicize the impact.
- When you compromise, and it works, acknowledge it.
- When your predictions prove accurate, remind stakeholders.

Build relationships:

- Involve stakeholders early (Chapter 8's progressive involvement).
- Respect the constraints they face.
- Help them succeed in their goals.

When you've built capital through successful collaboration, stakeholders trust you when you say, "This compromise is too far—we need to find another way."

Calibrating Push-Back to UX Maturity

How hard you push depends on organizational maturity:

Ad-hoc maturity:

- **Pick battles carefully:** You have limited capital

- **Frame push-back around business risk:** "This creates a support burden we can't sustain."
- **Offer alternatives:** Don't just say no, propose viable options
- **Build credibility first:** Prove UX value with quick wins before fighting big battles

Defined maturity:

- **Push back on violations of established process:** "We agreed to test before shipping—skipping testing violates our process."
- **Frame around user research:** "Users clearly told us this wouldn't work. Here's the data."
- **Engage stakeholders in solving:** "Engineering says it's complex. Let's workshop alternatives together."

Managed/Optimizing maturity:

- **Push back on strategic misalignment:** "This contradicts our product strategy."
- **Frame around long-term vision:** "This short-term fix creates long-term problems."
- **Propose strategic alternatives:** "Here's how we could achieve business goals AND serve users well."

The strategic decision: The same push-back delivered wrong for the maturity level damages your credibility. Calibrate your approach to what your organization is ready to hear.

Moving Forward into Phase 1

You now understand the five-phase toolkit-building process and how it operationalizes the six principles from Chapter 4.

We'll start where all strategic toolkit-building must start—with an honest assessment of your context.

Because choosing tools before understanding context is like buying equipment before knowing what kind of work you need to do. You might get lucky, but you're far more likely to waste money on tools you can't use and miss tools you desperately need.

Let's assess your reality so you know which tools to put in your toolkit.

PHASE 1

Assess Context

"Reality is that which, when you stop believing in it, doesn't go away." — **Philip K. Dick**

"Your EdTech constraints are those which, when you ignore them in research planning, still sink your project." — **Philip K. Dick (adapted)**

Strategic research starts with one question: "What's actually true about our situation?"

Not "what do we wish were true?" or "what works at other companies?" but "what constraints and opportunities do we have?"

I've watched teams skip this step. They jump straight to method selection—"Let's do user interviews!" or "We should run a Design Sprint!"—without first understanding whether those methods fit their reality.

The result? Research that can't influence decisions because the timing is wrong. Insights that can't be implemented because technical constraints weren't considered. Months-long studies when stakeholders needed answers in weeks.

The scenarios in Chapter 5 showed how different companies and their unique contexts informed my tool selection. This chapter shows you how to assess two contextual layers—organizational and EdTech-specific—to determine which tools will actually work in your situation.

The Two Context Layers

Before choosing any research method, assess two layers:

Layer 1: Organizational Context. Your internal reality (maturity, roadmap, technical constraints)

Layer 2: EdTech-Specific Context. Industry constraints covered in Part 1 (timing, users, access, politics)

Both layers interact. Your organizational maturity affects which EdTech constraints you can navigate. Your roadmap flexibility determines whether seasonal access creates problems or just requires adaptation.

Let's walk through how to assess each layer strategically.

Layer 1: Organizational Context

Three factors shape what research approaches your organization can actually support: UX maturity, roadmap flexibility, and technical reality. For each factor, you'll answer assessment questions, then translate your answers into strategic implications for method selection.

UX Maturity: What Will Your Organization Value and Use?

This isn't about judging your organization. It's about understanding what research approaches will be understood and acted upon.

<u>Assessment questions:</u>

- How does leadership currently view UX?
    - Making things pretty?
    - Solving user problems?
    - Strategic advantage?
    - Executing on ideas they've handed down?
- What happens to research insights?
    - Inform decisions?
    - Get presented, then ignored?
    - Never requested in the first place?
- Do you have established research processes?
    - Repeatable practices?
    - Ad-hoc as needed?
    - Nothing yet?
- How do stakeholders react to user research?
    - Trust it?
    - Question it?
    - Don't understand it?
    - Make decisions even if it's in opposition?

<u>Strategic implications by maturity level:</u>

Ad-hoc: Research and UX strategy not yet valued → Need quick wins proving UX worth before comprehensive research

- **Can't sustain** Continuous Discovery, Disruptive Research, and long timeline studies
- **Should focus on:** Heuristic evaluations, analytics, and low-cost improvements with measurable impact
- **Success looks like:** Building credibility so you can propose deeper research during the next cycle

Defined: Building UX function, establishing processes → Can invest in research but has yet to build stakeholder understanding

- **Can sustain:** Structured research projects with clear timelines and deliverables
- **Should focus on:** Helping stakeholders understand how to use research, building repeatable practices
- **Success looks like:** Stakeholders requesting research and knowing what to do with the findings

Managed: Research integrated into product development → Can implement sophisticated approaches (adapted for EdTech)

- **Can sustain:** Regular research cadence, stakeholder participation in synthesis
- **Should focus on:** Optimizing efficiency and scaling impact across the organization
- **Success looks like:** Research that informs decisions consistently and stakeholders who are fluent in research thinking

Optimizing: Research shapes strategic direction → Can pursue strategic initiatives.

- **Can sustain:** Long-term research investments, category-defining insights
- **Should focus on:** Driving innovation, competitive differentiation through UX
- **Success looks like:** UX influencing company strategy, not just product features

---

The strategic decision: Don't choose methods your organization isn't ready to value—because even if you knock those methods out of the park, it's unlikely to have any impact. Build maturity progressively.

Roadmap Flexibility: Can Research Actually Influence What Gets Built?

This determines whether you should do generative research (discovering new directions) or evaluative research (optimizing existing plans).

<u>Assessment questions:</u>

- What's committed for the next 6–12 months?
    - Everything?
    - Major features?
    - General direction only?
- What drives roadmap decisions?
    - Enterprise contracts?
    - Leadership intuition?
    - User research?
    - Market analysis?
- How far ahead are commitments made?
    - Quarters?
    - Years?
- Can research change priorities within planning cycles?
    - Shift quarterly focus?
    - Adjust sprint priorities?
    - Can't change anything?

<u>Strategic implications by flexibility level:</u>

Completely locked: Roadmap committed 6–12-plus months based on contracts/investors

- **Don't waste time on:** Generative research discovering new opportunities (can't act on them)
- **Focus research on:** Optimizing execution of committed work (usability testing, workflow refinement, incremental improvements)
- **Method selection:** Evaluative methods that improve what's being built anyway

Somewhat flexible: Quarterly adjustments possible, can influence priorities within planning windows.

- **Time research to:** Quarterly planning cycles (generate insights before planning, inform next quarter)
- **Balance:** Evaluative research (improve current work) + some generative research (inform upcoming quarters)
- **Method selection:** A mix of optimization and discovery that is timed strategically

Highly responsive: Research can drive pivots and change direction.

- **Can pursue:** Generative research, strategic discovery, category-defining insights
- **Focus on:** Identifying opportunities, validating strategic bets
- **Method selection:** Full range of methods available, choose based on the question being answered

---

The strategic decision: Match research type to roadmap reality. Locked roadmaps need optimization research. Flexible roadmaps can benefit from discovery research.

Don't think a locked roadmap means it will always be that way. By building UX maturity in the organization, you can shift towards a more responsive roadmap as stakeholders see the impact research can make.

Technical Reality: What Can You Actually Build?

This determines whether to research ideal solutions or solutions constrained by architecture.

Assessment questions:

- How old is your codebase?
    - Built this year?
    - Five years ago?
    - Over ten years ago?
- What's required to make major changes?
    - Modify existing components?
    - Build new patterns?
    - Rebuild platform architecture?
- How often do "unbuildable" design ideas emerge?
    - Never?
    - Occasionally?
    - Frequently?
- What's the relationship between design and engineering?
    - Collaborative partnership?

- o Adversarial?
- o Designers don't understand technical constraints?
- o Engineers don't participate in understanding user needs and just build from requirements thrown over the wall to them?

<u>Strategic implications by technical debt level:</u>

High debt: Legacy systems, 10–20 years of code, platform constraints

- **Factor into research:** Technical constraints from day one (don't discover unbuildable solutions)
- **Research questions:** "Given our architecture, what's the best solution?" not "What's the ideal solution?"
- **Build a business case:** When the user needs to justify a technical investment to unlock better solutions
- **Method selection:** Involve engineering early, prototype within a feasible space

Moderate debt: Some constraints, but strategic technical investments can expand possibilities.

- **Research both:** Near-term solutions (buildable now) + strategic opportunities (worth technical investment)
- **Decision framework:** User value vs. technical investment required
- **Method selection:** Standard approaches work, but validate technical feasibility during design

Low debt: Modern architecture, few technical constraints.

- **Research freely:** Ideal solutions without technical limitations

- **Focus on:** User value, not buildability (technical feasibility rarely blocks good ideas)
- **Method selection:** Full range of approaches viable

The strategic decision: Don't discover perfect solutions you can't build. Either research within constraints or explicitly research opportunities worth investment to unlock.

I want to be clear here: I'm not saying you can't advocate for a rebuild if that's what you believe is best for the users and the long-term health of the product and business. I've successfully advocated for rebuilds on three separate occasions.

One was to move us away from a third-party platform that we'd outgrown the functionality of, which decreased our ability to be nimble, as we had to go through them for all changes. Another was a complete rebuild when I wasn't even hired as a UX professional because I saw just how bad the product was and gathered enough evidence to convince my bosses that it was essential if they wanted the tool to be used at all by districts in the state. A third was when a portion of the product was slated to be moved off an old platform for tech-debt reasons (it was a drain on time for engineering to continue to maintain), and I didn't want it to be rebuilt in the same way (with all the same UX problems), just on the newer platform.

Layer 2: EdTech-Specific Context

Part 1 (Chapters 1–3) explained what these constraints are and why they misalign with standard frameworks. This section shows you how to assess which constraints apply to your situation and what that means for method selection.

Sales Cycle Stage: When Must Decisions Be Made?

Your assessment:

- When do purchasing decisions happen in your market?
- When must your product be ready?
- What happens if you miss the window?

<u>Strategic implications:</u>

Adoption season approaching (within six months): Timeline is non-negotiable.

- **Research scope:** Only what can inform this launch (comprehensive discovery might miss the window).
- **Confidence threshold:** High enough to ship, not perfect (80–90 percent, depending on risk).
- **Method selection:** Fast-to-insight approaches, strategic sampling, and parallel research streams. Usability testing and iteration cycles of prototypes are important so that you don't release something that doesn't meet user needs, and that they're stuck with for the year.

Full cycle runway (6–12 months until next adoption window): Time allows strategic depth.

- **Research scope:** Can pursue comprehensive discovery and multiple iteration cycles.
- **Confidence threshold:** Can aim for 90 percent-plus confidence through thorough validation.

- **Method selection:** Time for generative research identifying new opportunities, deep user observation, multiple rounds of prototype testing and refinement, building in time for both teacher access windows (summer) and synthesis/design work (school year).
- **Strategic advantage:** Use the full cycle to research deeply, design thoughtfully, and validate thoroughly before committing to launch.

The strategic decision: Don't fight EdTech's seasonal reality. Use the time you have strategically—compress when you must, go deep when you can.

Three-User Dynamics: Who Actually Controls Adoption?

Your assessment:

- Who makes purchasing decisions?
- Who controls whether the product gets used?
- Who are you primarily designing for?
- What happens if one user type fails?

Strategic implications by control pattern:

Teachers control adoption:

- **Prioritize:** Teacher research over student research when resources are limited, and there's reason to believe teachers are unhappy with their experience

- **Remember:** Student experience matters, but the teacher is the gatekeeper
- **Risk:** Brilliant student content that teachers won't assign = wasted development

Admins control adoption (district mandates, compliance tools):

- **Prioritize:** Admin research for purchasing drivers
- **Also research:** Teacher and student experience (affects adoption quality and fidelity, even if mandated)
- **Success metric:** Minimal compliance use vs. enthusiastic adoption

Complex dynamics (multiple stakeholders with veto power):

- **Research:** All three user types and understand how their needs interact
- **Synthesize:** Identify conflicts between user types, make strategic trade-offs
- **Design priority:** Usually the gatekeeper, but validate the full workflow chain

---

The strategic decision: Research the user who controls adoption (not just purchasing decisions) first. Don't only research end users when gatekeepers determine whether your product gets used.

Lock-In Reality: How Much Can Users Tolerate "Minimum Viable?"

Your assessment:

- How long are users committed once they adopt?
- What's the switching cost if users hate your product?
- How will users perceive mid-year changes?
- What's your iteration window?

<u>Strategic implications:</u>

High lock-in (9-month school year, can't switch):

- **Confidence needed:** 85–90 percent before launch (can't iterate based on feedback if users hate it)
- **Validation approach:** Thorough pre-launch testing
- **Mid-year changes:** Only non-disruptive improvements (bug fixes, performance, subtle refinements)
- **Method selection:** Deep validation before launch, not rapid iteration after

Moderate lock-in (semester/quarter-based):

- **Confidence needed:** 75–85 percent before launch
- **Iteration windows:** Semester breaks for workflow changes
- **Method selection:** Balance pre-launch validation with planned iteration points

Low lock-in (voluntary adoption, easy switching):

- **Confidence needed:** 65–75 percent is sufficient to launch
- **Iteration approach:** More traditional MVP thinking is viable
- **Method selection:** Can use Lean approaches that don't work with high lock-in

---

The strategic decision: Higher lock-in requires higher confidence before launch. Don't ship "minimum viable" when users can't leave (or won't tolerate frequent UX changes) for nine months.

Access Barriers: When Can You Actually Talk to Users?

Your assessment:

- When are teachers available for research?
- What's required to research students?
- How long do approval processes take?
- Who else can provide insights when primary users are unavailable?
- What's your budget (both in money for incentives and time for employees to spend on research)?

<u>Strategic implications by access pattern:</u>

Seasonal teacher access only (most common):

- **Research timing:** Batch intensive research in summer (June–August)
- **School-year approach:** Analytics, admin interviews, existing data during September–May
- **Method selection:** Can't assume weekly access
- **Plan ahead:** Summer research must inform full-year decisions

Student research requires IRB (K–12 contexts, if required by the state or district):

- **Lead time:** Start processes 3–6 months before you need access

- **Backup plans:** What if approval is delayed or denied?
- **Method selection:** Can't rely on rapid student testing for quick decisions
- **Alternative sources:** Teacher perspectives, analytics, and proxy testing with adults

Year-round access possible (some EdTech contexts, higher ed):

- **Research timing:** Flexible, can adapt to Continuous Discovery approaches
- **Method selection:** Broader range of approaches viable
- **Still consider:** Seasonal capacity changes (teachers are still busier during the school year)

The strategic decision: Match research cadence to access reality. Batch research when users are available, use alternative sources when they're not.

Political and Regulatory Landscape: What Constraints Are Non-Negotiable?

Your assessment:

- What regulatory requirements apply?
- What approval processes exist?
- What do funding sources require?
- How do these constraints affect design decisions?

<u>Strategic implications:</u>

Heavy regulatory constraints (government, Title I, approved lists):

- **Research focus:** User needs that meet compliance requirements (not just user needs)
- **Design constraints:** Must satisfy regulatory requirements regardless of user preference
- **Method selection:** Factor compliance into research from day one
- **Success metric:** User-centered design within required constraints

Moderate political hurdles (district approval, board sign-off):

- **Research scope:** Include stakeholder perspectives beyond end users
- **Build a case for:** Both user value and political viability
- **Method selection:** Multi-stakeholder research, strategic framing

Minimal constraints (direct school relationships, private customers):

- **Research focus:** User needs drive decisions
- **Design freedom:** Broader solution space possible
- **Method selection:** User-centered approaches without heavy constraint mapping

---

The strategic decision: Don't research ideal solutions that violate compliance requirements. Factor non-negotiable constraints into research from the start.

Common Context Assessment Mistakes

Even experienced practitioners fall into these traps:

Mistake 1: "This Framework Worked at My Last Company"

What happens: You bring a framework from B2B SaaS or consumer tech and assume it'll work in EdTech, so you skip context assessment entirely. Or, you assume what worked at your last EdTech company will work here as well.

Why it fails: You've read this far, so you know that using the same framework for completely different contexts is malpractice.

Strategic shift: Assess current context first. Then adapt framework elements that fit. Don't assume portability.

Mistake 2: Assuming Who You're Designing For = Who Controls Adoption

What happens: You focus research on end users (students) because that feels right or feels flashier to sell, and ignore the gatekeepers (teachers).

Why it fails: This may sound familiar. Brilliant student features that teachers won't assign never get used. You've optimized for users with zero adoption control.

Strategic shift: A context assessment reveals who controls adoption. That's who you should research first, even if they're not the end user.

Mistake 3: "We'll Do Comprehensive Research, Then Decide"

What happens: You plan thorough, rigorous research without checking timeline constraints or roadmap flexibility.

Why it fails: Perfect research delivered too late has zero impact. If your roadmap can't change, research that identifies new directions just burns time and budget on insights you can't use.

Strategic shift: A context assessment reveals the required confidence level and available timeline. Set the confidence threshold first, then choose the fastest path to that confidence.

Mistake 4: "Research Should Be Unbiased by Constraints"

What happens: You research ideal solutions without considering classroom realities, technical debt, or regulatory requirements.

Why it fails: You discover ideal solutions you can't actually build. Research insights that ignore constraints become shelf-ware, not shipped products.

Strategic shift: Understand feasibility constraints upfront. Research within a realistic possibility space, or explicitly research strategic opportunities worth major investment.

Putting Context Assessment Into Practice

Context assessment isn't a lengthy process. It's strategic thinking that shapes everything else.

Here's what it looks like:

The Context Assessment Questions

Before choosing ANY research method, ask yourself:

Organizational Reality:

- What's our UX maturity? (Will this research approach be valued and used?)
- How locked is our roadmap? (Can research actually influence what gets built?)
- What's our technical reality? (Can we build what we might discover users need?)

EdTech-Specific Reality:

- When do decisions need to be made? (Does that align with when we can access users?)
- Who controls adoption? (Are we researching the right user type?)
- What's our lock-in reality? (How confident must we be before launch?)
- When can we access users? (Does our method require access we don't have?)
- What political/regulatory constraints exist? (Are we researching within a feasible space?)

Output: Clear understanding of which methods will work and which won't, given your specific reality.

Moving Forward to Tool Selection

You now understand how to assess the two context layers:

Organizational context tells you what research approaches your organization can value and use (maturity), whether research can influence direction (roadmap flexibility), and what's technically buildable (debt level).

EdTech-specific context tells you when decisions must be made (sales cycles), who controls adoption (three-user dynamics), how much users can tolerate "minimum viable" (lock-in), when you can access users (barriers), and what constraints are non-negotiable (political/regulatory).

Next question: "Given our situation, which methods get us to confident decisions fastest?"

That's Phase 2: Strategic tool and artifact selection.

In Chapter 7, you'll learn how to use your context assessment to make informed decisions about:

- Which research methods fit your reality
- How to set appropriate confidence thresholds
- Which communication artifacts will drive decisions with your stakeholders
- When to use fast validation versus deep discovery

Context assessment is the foundation. Tool selection is where that foundation pays off.

→ For detailed context mapping worksheets that systematically walk you through these assessment questions with your specific situation, check my free resources available at kellymorganux.com.

PHASE 2

Select Tools and Artifacts

"For every complex problem there is an answer that is clear, simple, and wrong." — **H.L. Mencken**

"For every EdTech constraint there is a research method that is popular, comprehensive, and completely inappropriate." — **H.L. Mencken (adapted)**

You've assessed your context. You understand your organizational maturity, roadmap flexibility, technical constraints, and EdTech-specific realities.

Now for the strategic question: "Which tools should I select for my toolkit given our reality?"

This chapter shows you how to think about tool selection strategically by:

1. matching research type to your question
2. choosing tools that fit your EdTech context
3. designing communication artifacts that drive decisions
4. knowing when to validate fast versus when to go deep

Remember from Chapter 4: Frameworks are pre-built toolboxes. You're building your own toolkit by selecting tools that fit *your* context. This chapter shows you how to make those selections strategically.

A Note on Method Mechanics and Biases

This chapter focuses on strategic method selection: determining which approaches fit your context and goals. I'm assuming you understand research mechanics and method biases. But if you need tactical execution guidance, see *Continuous Discovery Habits* by Teresa Torres, *Disruptive Research* by Debbie Levitt and Larry Marine, resources from the Nielsen Norman Group, or *The Strategic UX Toolkit Playbook*.

One critical strategic principle: Triangulate using multiple methods with different biases so they cancel out rather than compound. If interviews suggest teachers want feature X but analytics show they don't use similar existing features, that tension is valuable data.

Generative vs. Iterative Research: Know What You're Solving For

Before you choose any specific research method, you need to understand what type of research question you're answering. Are you discovering unmet needs or optimizing existing solutions?

Real discovery research requires a different approach.

Generative Research: Finding Unmet Needs

Generative research (also called discovery or disruptive research) can't happen if you start with existing products—yours or competitors'.

Here's why: If you observe users with existing products, ask about their experiences with current tools, or analyze what competitors built, you're working within the assumption that existing solutions address the right problems. You might improve those solutions. You might find better ways to solve those problems. But you'll never discover the needs that no product has addressed yet.

To break out of the box, go solution-agnostic. Watch or talk to people in analog settings. How do teachers manage classrooms without your product? What tasks are they trying to complete? What are their actual goals, not just what your product category claims they need? What workarounds or aids have they created for themselves?

Observing analog workflows is how you find unmet needs—problems that existing products haven't realized are the actual problems to solve.

When generative research fits:

- Redesigning a product completely
- Moving into new or expanding markets
- Expanding the current product into new problem spaces
- When you have time and the organizational patience for strategic insights (remember Chapter 6's context—optimizing maturity so that organizations can sustain this, while ad-hoc maturity can't)

Methods that work:

- Contextual observation in real environments (classrooms, not conference rooms)
- Solution-agnostic interviews ("How do you accomplish X without any tools?")
- Task analysis watching analog workflows

Iterative Research: Optimizing What Exists

You're not always trying to disrupt markets. Sometimes you've already done generative research and discovered the problem. Your product addresses that problem. But no product is perfect.

That's where iterative research comes in. Iterative research improves existing products by uncovering what the problems are and why they're problems, which tells you how to fix them.

The two-phase iterative approach:

Phase 1: "What is the problem?"

This is straightforward, often inexpensive, and easy. Usage analytics, support requests, training summaries, surveys, and heuristic evaluations— all great at uncovering where problems exist. Where do users drop off? Where do they get stuck? What features cause issues?

Phase 2: "Why is this a problem and how should we fix it?"

This is more time-intensive and can't be figured out with analytics. Moderated usability testing lets you probe when users aren't explaining their thinking. You need to understand why they're doing what they're doing to know how to fix it.

At one company, we subscribed to a user analytics tool that included screen recordings of user interactions. An executive told me that this capability would replace the need to do user interviews or classroom observations (as there wasn't a budget for those things). Watching those recordings was a great way to find where a problem existed, but it did very little to answer the "why" or "how we should fix it." Yes, we could see everything the user was doing in the product, but we had no idea what their context was. What had the teacher instructed the students to do? Is that why the student isn't following our intended learning progression path? Are students working together? Is the teacher right there helping the student? What was the teacher's goal when they were fumbling with their interface? Without context, there's no way to understand why the user was struggling and how we could best fix it.

The good news: You don't need to talk to very many people. Patterns emerge quickly in well-designed iterative research.

When iterative research fits:

- Improving existing designs
- Fixing pain points or problems with current features
- Your context has locked roadmaps (remember Chapter 6—in that context, you can only optimize what you're already building)

Methods for "What is the problem?"

- Analytics (usage patterns, drop-off points)
- Heuristic evaluation (expert review against known principles)
- Surveys (where users struggle)
- Observation (watching task completion)—including screen recordings via analytics tools
- Support requests

Methods for "Why and how to fix it?"

- User interviews
- Moderated usability testing (can probe for thinking)
- Desk research on best practices
- Competitor analysis (how others solved similar problems)
- Observations or field studies

> **Strategic decision:** Match research type to what
> you're actually trying to learn. Apply discovery
> research when you're identifying unmet needs and
> have time to act on disruptive insights. Use iterative
> research when you're optimizing what exists or when
> roadmap flexibility doesn't support strategic pivots.

Strategic Tool Selection: Existing Sources First

Before scheduling new research, mine the data you already have.

I've watched teams plan elaborate research efforts without checking what existing sources could answer their questions faster. Support tickets, sales calls, onboarding surveys, product analytics—all sitting there unused while teams debate which research tools to deploy.

This is why ResearchOps and qualitative data repositories are so important! I've worked in many places where data is spread across different teams and can't be easily searched, synthesized, and analyzed.

Support tickets show which features consistently confuse users and problems severe enough that users seek help.

Sales calls reveal what drives purchasing decisions, features customers demand, and objections that block deals.

Onboarding surveys and NPS comments contain rich qualitative data that teams often ignore because they focus on the scores. The comments often matter more than the numbers.

Mid-year reviews meeting recordings provide great insight into customer pain points as they started implementing (or reasons they already stopped the implementation).

Product analytics show behavior—where users go, where they get stuck, what they never use.

Previous research from 6–18 months ago often contains findings that still apply or patterns that have worsened.

The strategic combination:

Use existing sources to:

1. prioritize research topics (tickets + analytics + sales feedback reveal the biggest problems)
2. form hypotheses (existing data suggests possible reasons)
3. design better questions (you already know the "what," now focus new research on the "why")
4. triangulate findings (if interviews, tickets, and analytics all point to the same problem, confidence increases)

The strategic decision: Don't choose between existing sources and new research tools. Combine them strategically—existing sources show where to focus. New research tools reveal why problems exist and how to fix them.

Understanding Specific Research Methods in EdTech Context

Not all research methods work equally well in EdTech. Some are powerful tools you'll use constantly. Others sound appealing but fail given EdTech's unique constraints.

Here's a practical guide to common methods—what they're good for, what they're not, and EdTech-specific considerations.

Quantitative Methods

<u>Analytics</u>

What it tells you: Where users go, where they get stuck, what they never use, patterns across many users

When to use:

- Identifying which problems to prioritize (high-frequency pain points)
- Validating whether solutions worked (before/after comparison)
- Understanding usage patterns across user segments

EdTech considerations:

- **Seasonal patterns matter:** September usage looks different than May usage—don't compare across seasons without accounting for context.
- **Three-user analytics:** Track admin, teacher, and student behaviors separately—aggregated metrics hide crucial adoption patterns.

- **Implementation lag:** Teachers might not use features until weeks after launch, when they have time to learn them—don't judge adoption in the first week.
- **Limitations:** Analytics show *what* is happening, not *why*. You'll need qualitative methods to understand the causes.

<u>Surveys</u>

What it tells you: Self-reported preferences, satisfaction levels, awareness of features, demographic patterns

When to use:

- Reaching many users quickly across distributed locations
- Prioritizing which problems affect most users
- Tracking satisfaction trends over time (NPS, CSAT)

EdTech considerations:

- **Timing affects response rates:** Don't survey teachers in September-October (overwhelmed) or late May (checked out).
- **Keep it SHORT:** Teachers don't have fifteen minutes—aim for 3–5 minutes maximum.
- **Comments matter more than scores:** The NPS number is less valuable than understanding *why* teachers would/wouldn't recommend.

Limitations:

- Self-reported data is unreliable. What people say they do rarely matches what they actually do.
- Can't explore nuance or probe for deeper understanding.

- Response bias: People who respond aren't representative of all users.

The strategic decision: Use surveys to identify problem areas and gauge sentiment. Use qualitative methods to understand why problems exist and how to fix them.

Qualitative Methods

<u>One-on-One Interviews</u>

What it tells you: Detailed understanding of user contexts, goals, pain points, workarounds, and decision-making

When to use:

- Understanding workflows and task contexts
- Exploring motivations and emotional dimensions
- Discovering problems you didn't know to look for

EdTech considerations:

- **Summer access window:** Plan most interviews for June–August when teachers have capacity.
- **30–45 minutes maximum:** Even in summer, respect their time.
- **Compensate appropriately:** $50–75 for forty-five minutes acknowledges their professional value.
- **All three user types:** Interview admins, teachers, AND students (with proper permissions) to understand the full adoption chain.

Limitations:

- Time-intensive (recruiting, conducting, synthesizing)
- Small sample size—need other methods to validate patterns apply broadly
- What people say they do doesn't always match actual behavior

---

The strategic decision: Interviews are your primary tool for understanding *why* problems exist and what outcomes users actually need. Pair with analytics to validate patterns.

Focus Groups

What it tells you: Group dynamics, shared experiences, areas of consensus and disagreement

When to use: Rarely. One-on-one interviews almost always work better.

EdTech considerations:

- **Groupthink risk:** Teachers may not share honest feedback about district-mandated tools in group settings.
- **Dominant voices:** One outspoken participant can skew the entire discussion.
- **Scheduling nightmare:** Getting 6–8 teachers available simultaneously is nearly impossible.

Limitations:

- Group dynamics suppress individual perspectives
- Can't dive deep into any one person's experience

- More time to organize than individual interviews
- Analysis is more complex—need to track who said what and account for social pressure

---

The strategic decision: Skip focus groups in favor of individual interviews unless you specifically need to observe group dynamics or build consensus among stakeholders.

Observations / Field Studies

What it tells you: How users actually behave in their real environment, not how they describe their behavior

When to use:

- Discovering workflows you wouldn't learn about from interviews
- Understanding the classroom/district context that affects product usage
- Finding unmet needs through solution-agnostic observation

EdTech considerations:

- **Classroom access requires permissions:** IRB, district approval, principal buy-in, teacher cooperation
- **School year only:** Can't observe classroom usage in summer— plan 3–6 months ahead
- **Disruptive presence:** Being in classrooms can change teacher behavior (Hawthorne effect)
- **Time-intensive:** One hour of observation generates hours of synthesis

Limitations:

- Logistically complex in EdTech
- Presence changes behavior
- Can only observe when users are actually using the product

The strategic decision: Observations and field studies are powerful for generative research to discover unmet needs, but plan lead time and use it strategically—not for every project.

Task Analysis

What it tells you: The steps users take to accomplish goals, decision points, and the knowledge required at each step.

When to use:

- Designing new workflows
- Understanding where current workflows break down
- Mapping knowledge gaps your product needs to fill

EdTech considerations:

- **Watch analog workflows:** How do teachers roster students without your product? What workarounds exist?
- **Seasonal variations:** End-of-year workflows differ from beginning-of-year workflows. Account for timing.
- **Multi-user task chains:** Teacher assigns → Student completes → Admin reviews reports. Map the complete chain.

Limitations:

- Doesn't tell you *why* users do things in certain ways
- It can be time-intensive to map completely
- Workflows vary by user context

The strategic decision: Task analysis is essential for task-based design (Chapter 10). Pair with interviews to understand both *what* users do and *why* they do it that way.

Design and Usability Testing Methods

5-Second Testing

What it tells you: First impressions, visual hierarchy, what stands out immediately

When to use:

- Testing whether key information is immediately visible
- Validating visual hierarchy before detailed design
- Comparing design alternatives quickly

EdTech considerations:

- **Good for:** Testing whether important elements (like "Save" confirmation) are noticed immediately.
- **Not sufficient for:** Validating complete workflows. Teachers need to accomplish tasks, not just have good impressions.

Limitations:

- Tests recognition, not task completion
- Doesn't account for real usage context
- Can't replace comprehensive usability testing

The strategic decision: Use 5-second testing as a quick check on visual hierarchy, but don't rely on it alone. EdTech products need task completion validation.

<u>A/B Testing</u>

What it tells you: Which version performs better on specific metrics (clicks, conversions, time-on-task).

When to use in EdTech: Almost never.

Why A/B testing fails in EdTech:

- **Built for conversion optimization:** A/B testing assumes you're optimizing funnel metrics. EdTech products optimize for learning outcomes and teacher efficiency, not conversion rates.
- **Requires high traffic for statistical significance**: A/B testing works for consumer products with millions of users, not EdTech products with smaller user bases.
- **Lock-in periods prevent switching:** You can't iterate based on results if the users are locked in for nine months.
- **Three-user dynamics:** Optimizing for one user type may harm another. A/B tests can't account for adoption chain effects.

- **Seasonal confounds:** September usage differs from May usage, making it hard to isolate what's actually being tested vs. a seasonal variation.
- **Ethical considerations:** A/B testing that might affect student learning raises ethical concerns—the same concerns that drive IRB approval requirements for educational research.

What to use instead:

- **Usability testing:** Validate designs before launch with 5–8 strategic users
- **Pre/post comparison:** Launch to all users at the appropriate time, measure before/after metrics
- **Cohort analysis:** Compare usage patterns across different user segments or time periods

---

The strategic decision: A/B testing solves conversion problems. EdTech has adoption problems. Use methods designed for understanding adoption dynamics instead.

Expectation Testing

What it tells you: What users expect to happen vs. what actually happens

When to use:

- Validating interaction patterns match user mental models
- Testing whether labels and icons communicate intent
- Discovering mismatches between design and expectations

EdTech considerations:

- **Mental model gaps:** Teachers expect your product to work like their LMS. Test whether your patterns match those expectations.
- **Domain-specific expectations:** What "rostering" means varies by district. Validate terminology matches your users' language.

Limitations:

- Only tells you about expectations, not whether users can actually complete tasks
- Doesn't replace comprehensive task testing

The strategic decision: Use expectation testing early in design to validate terminology and interaction patterns, then follow with task completion testing.

<u>Icon Testing</u>

What it tells you: Whether icons communicate intended meaning without text labels

When to use:

- Validating icon choices before implementation
- Testing whether icons are recognizable to your specific user base
- Deciding whether icons need accompanying text

EdTech considerations:

- **Educational context matters:** Common consumer icons may not be recognized by all teachers.

- **Accessibility requirement:** WCAG requires text labels anyway, so icon-only interfaces won't pass compliance.

Limitations:

- Tests recognition in isolation, not in a real task context
- Domain knowledge affects results

The strategic decision: Icon testing is a quick validation tool, but remember, EdTech products need text labels for accessibility regardless of icon clarity.

First-Click Testing

What it tells you: Whether the initial action users should take is intuitive

When to use:

- Testing whether task entry points are obvious
- Validating information architecture
- Comparing design alternatives for clarity

EdTech considerations:

- **Critical for infrequent tasks:** License assignment happens 2–3 times per year. The first click must be obvious because teachers won't build muscle memory.
- **Cognitive load matters:** Teachers scanning quickly between classes need immediately obvious actions.

Limitations:

- Only tests the first action, not the complete workflow

- Doesn't account for what happens after the first click

The strategic decision: Pair first-click testing with task completion testing. The first click gets users started, but you need to validate that they can finish successfully.

Navigation Testing

What it tells you: Whether users can find content/features using your information architecture

When to use:

- Validating navigation structure before building
- Testing whether feature placement matches user mental models
- Comparing organizational schemes

EdTech considerations:

- **Three-user navigation needs:** Admins, teachers, and students need different things. Test navigation with each one separately.
- **Frequency affects findability:** Daily tasks need to be immediately accessible; infrequent tasks can be nested deeper.

Limitations:

- Tests findability in isolation, not in a real workflow context
- Doesn't validate whether features work once found

> **The strategic decision:** Navigation testing is essential for complex products, but it should be validated with task completion testing in realistic scenarios.

Preference Testing

What it tells you: Which design users prefer aesthetically

When to use: Sparingly, and only after usability is validated

Why preference testing is misleading:

- **Preference ≠ usability:** Users often prefer designs that are actually harder to use (e.g., flat design looks "cleaner" but takes 22 percent longer to identify actionable elements).
- **Beauty bias:** More polished designs get preference even if less functional.
- **Can't explain why:** Users rarely articulate meaningful reasons for preferences.

EdTech considerations:

- **Accessibility requirements dictate many choices:** Color contrast, text size, and interaction patterns must meet WCAG 2.2 AA regardless of preference.
- **Teacher time constraints:** Choose functional over beautiful when there's tension—teachers need efficiency, not aesthetics.

> **The strategic decision:** Use preference testing only after establishing that all options are equally usable.

Default to accessibility and task efficiency over aesthetic preferences.

Task Completion Testing (Usability Testing)

What it tells you: Whether users can successfully complete workflows, where they struggle, and what causes confusion.

When to use:

- Validating workflows before development
- Testing prototypes before committing to the final design
- Iterating on existing features with known problems

This is your primary validation tool in EdTech.

EdTech considerations:

- **Essential before launch:** High lock-in means you can't iterate after launch. Test thoroughly before shipping.
- **Test complete workflows:** Don't just test feature X in isolation. Test the teacher assigns → student completes → teacher reviews chain.
- **Realistic scenarios:** "Roster your students before school starts," not "click around the interface."
- **5–8 strategic users:** Patterns emerge quickly when participants are selected strategically.

Moderated vs. Unmoderated:

Moderated (live with researcher):

- **Pros:** Can probe for why, adjust tasks if unclear, catch nuance

- **Cons:** Scheduling nightmare, time-intensive, limited scale
- **EdTech fit:** Use for complex workflows or when "why" is critical

Unmoderated (recorded without researcher):

- **Pros:** Faster recruiting, participants do it on their schedule, and can reach more users
- **Cons:** Can't probe for understanding, task instructions must be perfect, can't course-correct
- **EdTech fit:** Use for focused feature testing or quick validation when the timeline is tight

---

The strategic decision: Usability testing is your highest-value validation tool in EdTech. Budget time for it. Test early (wireframes/prototypes) and often (after iterations). The cost of testing is trivial compared to shipping workflows that fail with locked-in users.

Triangulation: Combining Methods to Increase Confidence

Remember from the opening of this chapter: triangulate using multiple methods with different biases.

For feature adoption problems:

- Analytics (which features have low usage?)
- Support tickets (what do teachers say is confusing?)
- User interviews (why don't they use it?)
- Usability testing (can they complete the task when they try?)

For pre-launch validation:

- Task completion testing (can users complete workflows?)
- First-click testing (is the entry point obvious?)
- Analytics comparison (how does the new workflow perform vs. the old?)

For generative research:

- Observations (how do they solve problems now?)
- Task analysis (what steps do they take?)
- Interviews (what outcomes do they need?)

Different methods have different biases. Combining them gives you confidence that patterns are real, not the artifacts of one method's limitations.

> **The strategic decision:** Choose methods based on what you need to learn, your EdTech constraints (timing, access, lock-in), and the required confidence threshold. Don't choose methods because they're trendy or because you've always done it that way. Choose methods that fit your specific context.

Strategic Tool Selection by EdTech Context

Your Chapter 6 context assessment revealed your constraints. Now let's translate those into tool selection decisions that actually work in EdTech.

The tools exist in various frameworks—user interviews, usability testing, analytics, journey mapping, opportunity mapping, and prototype testing.

Your job isn't to use all of them. It's to select the ones that fit your specific situation.

If You Have Seasonal Access Only

Don't fight this reality. Design around it.

Summer research intensive: This may be your window for deep discovery. 10–20 teacher interviews, contextual observation, comprehensive task analysis—anything requiring sustained teacher participation happens now. Plan summer research to answer the whole year's questions because you can't count on access again until next June.

School-year lightweight approaches: When teachers are unavailable, rely on analytics (what are they actually using?), support tickets (what are they consistently struggling with?), admin interviews (admins are more available year-round), and quick intercepts (five-minute check-ins, not sixty-minute deep-dives).

If Roadmap Is Locked

Your Chapter 6 assessment revealed that the roadmap is committed to 6-12 months. Research can't change direction—only optimize execution.

Match research type to roadmap reality. If you can't do generative research (discovering new opportunities you can't build), focus on iterative research (optimizing what's committed).

Methods that fit:

- Usability testing on existing flows
- Analytics prioritizing which problems matter most

- Heuristic evaluation (identify obvious issues in hours without user access)

If Users Are Involuntary

Your Chapter 6 assessment revealed that K–12 students don't choose products. Maybe the teachers don't either.

Research questions change when adoption is mandated.

Questions you can't ask:

- Would you use this? (They don't have a choice)
- Would you choose this over competitors? (Not relevant)

Questions you should ask:

- Does this reduce your time or add to your workload?
- Does this fit into your existing workflow or fight it?
- What problems does this create? What problems does it solve?

Methods that fit:

- Task completion studies (Can they accomplish the required task? How efficiently?)
- Workflow integration analysis (Does this fit existing processes?)
- Efficiency measurements (Time-on-task, error rates, cognitive load)

If You Have Three-User Dynamics

Your Chapter 6 assessment revealed that admins buy, teachers control adoption, and students are end users.

Separate research streams by user type, synthesize strategically.

Admin research:

- Why do you buy EdTech?
- What do you need to prove to your board?
- How do you measure success?

Teacher research:

- Does this fit your workflow?
- Does this save or cost you time?
- What would make you assign this?

Student research:

- Can you complete this task?
- Do you understand what you're supposed to do?
- Where do you get stuck?

Cross-stakeholder synthesis:

- How do insights connect?
- Where do user needs conflict?

The strategic decision: Research all three user types, but weigh your research investment toward whoever controls adoption. In most EdTech contexts, that's teachers—they're the gatekeepers who determine whether your product actually gets used, regardless of what admins purchased or how brilliant your student experience is.

Communication Artifact Selection

Your findings don't change. But how you communicate them should, depending on who's in the room.

I've watched brilliant research die because insights were presented in formats stakeholders couldn't use. Detailed journey maps executives didn't have time to parse. Raw user quotes that engineers couldn't connect to technical decisions.

Strategic artifact selection matches the format to the stakeholder needs and communication goals.

By Stakeholder Type

For executives: They need one-page summaries outlining how these insights will impact their business. "A 25 percent NPS increase correlating with $450K in estimated retention impact" gets budget approval. Comprehensive research decks don't.

For product managers: Their language is impact vs. effort framing. "High-impact change affecting 60 percent of users, ships in two weeks" vs. "Medium-impact affecting 20 percent, requires two months" gives them what they need to make prioritization decisions.

For engineers: They love workflow diagrams and technical feasibility discussions. Involve them early: "Here's the user workflow. Given our architecture, what's feasible?" They become UX advocates when you respect their constraints.

For designers: They need task flows, mental models, and design principle applications. You want to give them the raw material for translating insights into design patterns.

By Communication Goal

To build empathy: Show 90-second video clips demonstrating real user struggle (remember Chapter 4's Principle 6—show users, don't just quote them).

To align on problems: Provide current-state workflow diagrams to visually reveal gaps.

To validate direction: Create hi-fidelity prototypes that simulate the experience before building (essential in high lock-in contexts).

To secure buy-in: Provide executive one-pagers with ROI calculations that translate user needs into business language.

The strategic decision: Don't create artifacts because "that's what UX people do." Create artifacts that drive specific decisions you need stakeholders to make.

Fast Validation vs. Deep Discovery: Matching Method Intensity to Decision Criticality

One of the most important strategic decisions: When do you validate quickly, and when do you invest in comprehensive research?

Remember from Chapter 4: Not every decision requires the same confidence level. Strategic researchers match method intensity to what's actually at stake.

Choose Fast Validation When:

- Timeline is tight (days or weeks to decision, not months)
- Risk is moderate (not betting it all, somewhat reversible)

- Context is somewhat understood (validating hypothesis, not exploring unknown)
- Goal is optimization (improving existing, not discovering new)

Methods: Analytics + 3–5 strategic interviews + prototype testing with 3-5 users

Time: 1–3 weeks to a confident recommendation

Choose Deep Discovery When:

- Timeline permits (months available)
- Risk is high (major investment, strategic bet, serious consequences if wrong)
- Context is unknown (new market, new users, new problem space)
- Goal is innovation (uncovering unmet needs, category-defining insights)

Methods: 10–20 interviews across segments + contextual observation + multi-method triangulation + multiple validation rounds

Time: 2–6 months to a confident recommendation

Reality in EdTech: Usually Hybrid

Most EdTech research combines approaches strategically:

- Fast validation during tight windows
- Deep discovery when time allows
- Pragmatic balance (fast methods for most decisions, deep discovery for strategic questions only)

> **The strategic decision:** Match method intensity to
> decision criticality, not to what sounds rigorous.

Moving Forward to Execution

You now understand strategic method and artifact selection:

Research type (generative vs. iterative) matches what you're trying to learn and whether your context can act on disruptive insights.

Existing sources should be mined before scheduling new research. They prioritize topics, form hypotheses, and enable triangulation.

Tool selection flows from EdTech context. Seasonal access, roadmap flexibility, and user control dynamics shape which approaches work.

Stakeholder artifacts match format to needs. Executives need different types of communication than engineers do.

Method intensity matches decision criticality—fast validation for optimization, deep discovery for strategic bets.

Context assessed (Chapter 6). Methods selected (Chapter 7).

Next: How do we execute research that actually drives decisions?

That's Phase 3: Strategic execution while building stakeholder buy-in— executing fast but rigorously, involving stakeholders throughout (not surprise presentations), and using clips to make problems undeniable.

→ For tool comparison charts, decision trees, and artifact templates helping you systematically choose approaches for your specific context, see *The Strategic UX Toolkit Playbook* (available at kellymorganux.com).

PHASE 3

Execute Research and Build Buy-In

*"A picture is worth a thousand words". — **Unknown***

"A 90-second clip is worth a thousand stakeholder arguments". — ***Unknown (adapted)***

Context assessed. Tools selected. Now you need to execute research that actually drives decisions.

This chapter shows you how to execute fast but rigorously, recognize patterns quickly through strategic sampling, synthesize continuously instead of waiting until the end, involve stakeholders progressively so findings drive action, and use clips to make problems undeniable.

Fast-to-Insight Through Strategic Sampling

Here's a pattern I see: Teams default to interviewing a lot of people because that's what they learned in school or saw at a previous company. They don't ask whether that number fits their context or confidence threshold.

Or, they think that's what they need to do, but they don't have time and resources to do it, so they don't do any research at all and lean on the "we know what our users need" philosophy.

Strategic sampling isn't about cutting corners. It's about recognizing that patterns emerge quickly when you select participants strategically.

When Patterns Become Visible

In well-designed research, consistent themes usually emerge by interview five.

Not always—sometimes you need more, sometimes only three. But if you're hearing the same problems from five strategically different users (different experience levels, different contexts, different workflows), the pattern is real.

The strategic question isn't "Should we do five or thirty interviews?" It's "Do we see consistent patterns emerging, and is our current confidence level sufficient for this decision?"

Strategic Participant Selection

The reason patterns emerge quickly is strategic selection—not random sampling.

Segment by what matters for your question:

If you're researching teacher onboarding, segment by experience level (first-year teachers vs. veterans) and tech savviness (tech enthusiasts vs. tech-resistant). Those characteristics affect how users approach onboarding.

Focus segments on characteristics that actually affect your research question. Elementary vs. high school might not matter if the onboarding workflow is the same.

<u>Recruit for diversity within segments:</u>

Within "first-year teachers," include different subject areas, different school types, and different classroom structures. You want diverse perspectives within each segment.

<u>Watch for saturation:</u>

When interview five reveals the exact same themes as interviews 1–4 with no new insights, you're likely seeing a real pattern. When interview five introduces completely new themes, you need more participants.

Parallel Research Streams

Don't work sequentially when you can work in parallel.

When parallel streams work:

- Different user types don't require sequential learning (admin insights don't need to inform teacher questions)
- Different methods have different timelines (analytics immediately available, interviews require scheduling)
- One research stream has long wait times (IRB approval, approval processes)

When sequential makes sense:

- Early findings should inform later questions (teacher insights reveal what to ask students)

- Budget constraints require spreading costs over time
- You need to validate patterns from one user type before investigating another

---

The strategic decision: Identify which research streams can run simultaneously and which require sequential learning. Default to parallel work unless there's a compelling reason that findings from Stream A must inform questions in Stream B. Parallel execution respects EdTech's tight timelines without sacrificing rigor.

Rolling Synthesis: Patterns Visible During Research

Many teams conduct all interviews, then start analysis. By the time they synthesize findings, it's weeks after the last interview.

That's batch analysis. It works, but it's slow.

Strategic researchers use rolling synthesis—synthesizing continuously during research, not after it's complete.

Rolling synthesis is also helpful in continuing to refine the testing or interviews. I've talked with many professionals who are concerned with doing this, as they feel it compromises the research or testing protocols. Remember, we're not doing Ph.D. or chemist-level research here—we're learning and evolving as we go to maximize the effectiveness of the information we gather.

How Rolling Synthesis Works

After each interview:

- Debrief immediately (what did we just learn?)
- Update running themes document (what patterns are emerging?)
- Note quotes or moments that illustrate themes
- Identify gaps (what questions do we still have?)

By interview five:

- Patterns becoming visible (three or more participants mentioning the same themes)
- Can start sharing emerging insights with stakeholders (progressive communication, not waiting for final presentation)
- Can adjust interview protocol if missing something important

After final interview:

- Synthesis is 80 percent complete (not starting from scratch)
- Can deliver findings within days (not weeks later)
- Stakeholders have been seeing themes emerge progressively (no surprises in the formal presentation)

The strategic decision: Start synthesizing after interview one, not after interview twenty. Rolling synthesis gets you to insights faster, allows mid-course corrections when you're missing something important, and prevents stakeholder surprise by sharing emerging themes progressively. The time investment in daily/weekly synthesis saves weeks on the back end.

Recognizing Signal vs. Noise

Not everything users tell you is equally important. Strategic researchers distinguish between patterns worth acting on and individual preferences that aren't representative.

What Qualifies as a Signal (Act on This)

Repeated across three-plus participants independently

Not coached or as a result of leading questions, but separately mentioned by multiple users without prompting.

Confirmed by other data sources

Analytics show the same problem, support tickets mention it, and stakeholders recognize it from their experience.

Specific and concrete

Not vague complaints ("this is confusing") but specific struggles ("I can't tell if my changes saved because there's no confirmation message").

Tied to outcomes users need to achieve

Not just preferences ("I'd like a dark mode") but barriers to task completion ("I can't see the text in bright classrooms").

What Qualifies as Noise (Don't Over-Index)

Single participant's unique situation (even if it's a "big client")

One teacher with a workflow no one else mentioned, tied to their specific classroom setup.

Contradicted by other evidence

User says they want feature X, but analytics show they never use similar features when available.

Edge case not representative

Unusual configuration, rare use case, applies to 1 percent of users.

Requested feature masking underlying need

Remember from Chapter 4's Principle 3: Users often request features when they really need outcomes. Dig for the actual need.

The strategic decision: Before acting on feedback, ask "Is this a pattern affecting most users, or an outlier from one person's unique context?" Acting on a signal creates value. Acting on noise wastes development resources on features most users don't need.

EdTech-Specific Execution Considerations

Beyond general research best practices, EdTech has specific constraints affecting how you execute research using your selected tools.

You selected tools in Chapter 7 that fit your context. Now you need to deploy those tools in ways that respect EdTech's unique constraints.

Accessing Teachers Strategically

Teachers are busy and underpaid. Respect both realities.

Summer professional development windows: June–August is when teachers have capacity. Still respect their time: 30–45 minutes maximum, even in the summer.

Remote interviews: Give you geographic reach without travel burden. Easier for teachers to fit into their schedules.

Appropriate compensation: Teachers are underpaid. Pay $50–75 for a forty-five-minute interview to acknowledge the value of their time. Don't expect free participation from professionals already stretched thin.

Strategic scheduling: Conduct batch interviews when teachers are available. Don't spread ten interviews over ten weeks—do them in 2–3 weeks when access is available.

Student Research Within Constraints

Student research requires navigating regulatory and political hurdles.

IRB approval timeline (if required by the state or district): Three to six months from submission to approval. Plan ahead—start processes long before you need access.

Parental consent burden: Parental consent creates ongoing administrative overhead—forms in multiple languages, rolling consent collection, and permission management.

District permission: Expect to navigate political gatekeepers and potentially gain board approval. Build relationships with district research coordinators.

School-year access only: Since you can't observe students during the summer (they're not in school), plan student research for the fall–spring window.

Strategic implication: Student research requires more lead time and political navigation than teacher research. Factor this into timelines.

Progressive Stakeholder Involvement

Remember from Chapter 4's Principle 5: Research drives decisions when stakeholders feel ownership, not when you present polished findings they're hearing for the first time.

Here's exactly how ownership-building works in practice.

Before Research Begins: Get Input on Questions

Share your research plan with product managers, engineers, and designers. Ask:

- What questions, if answered, would give you confidence to move forward?
- Who should we talk to?
- What would convince you that this is worth prioritizing?

Why this matters: Stakeholders who helped shape research questions are committed to acting on answers before you even start.

When stakeholders help define what you're investigating, they've already decided the investigation matters. Presenting findings becomes confirmation, not persuasion.

During Research: Share Emerging Themes Weekly (or Sooner!)

Don't wait until synthesis is complete. Share what you're learning as you learn it.

"We found an interesting pattern: Four out of six teachers mentioned struggling with X."

"We're seeing consistent themes around Y—here's a clip illustrating it."

Why this matters: Progressive exposure prevents the "surprise problem" where stakeholders get defensive when hearing about findings for the first time in formal presentations.

When stakeholders watch patterns emerge over weeks, they process that information gradually. By presentation time, they've already thought through the implications, instead of reacting defensively to unexpected findings.

- **For tight timelines** (2–3 week research windows): Daily or every-other-day Slack updates with emerging themes
- **For longer research** (four-plus weeks): Weekly email summaries with key quotes or brief clips
- Keep it:
    - brief (2–3 bullets maximum)
    - specific (numbers and quotes)
    - forward-looking (what you're exploring next)

Mid-Research: Collaborative Synthesis Session

This is where ownership really builds.

Bring PMs, engineers, and designers together (ninety minutes) to review clips and identify patterns. Provide structure, but let them discover insights.

Format:

1. **Context setting** (five minutes): "Here's what we've been researching and why."
2. **Clip review** (thirty minutes): Watch 4–6 clips showing user struggles or successes.
3. **Pattern identification** (thirty minutes): "What themes are you seeing? What surprises you?"
4. **Implication discussion** (twenty-five minutes): "What does this mean for our roadmap?"

Why this matters: They don't just hear insights—they *create* them by participating in synthesis. Stakeholders feel they discovered insights, not that you're reporting conclusions.

Pre-Presentation: Individual Stakeholder Previews

Before formal presentations, have 15–30 minute individual conversations with key stakeholders to preview major findings.

- "Here's what we're seeing—does this match your experience?"
- "Are you surprised by anything?"
- "What questions do you have before we present to the broader group?"

Why this matters: Stakeholders have time to process findings before group discussions. The formal presentation becomes confirmation, not revelation. You also get to address concerns privately before they become public objections.

Who to preview with:

- Product managers (will this change roadmap priorities?)
- Engineering leads (is this technically feasible?)
- Key executives (will this get budget/resources?)
- Designers (does this align with design direction?)

Individual conversations let stakeholders process without performing for a group. They can ask "dumb questions" privately. They can raise concerns without appearing to block progress publicly.

The Presentation: Confirmation, Not Revelation

By this point, stakeholders already know the findings because they've been involved throughout.

The presentation confirms what they've been tracking. No surprises.

Structure:

1. **Remind them of the journey** (five minutes): "You helped us define the research questions. You've been seeing themes emerge weekly. Today we're synthesizing what we learned together."
2. **Show 2–3 clips** (ten minutes): Illustrate key findings visually.
3. **Present patterns** (fifteen minutes): The themes they've already been tracking, now organized and synthesized.
4. **Discuss implications** (twenty minutes): What should we do about this?

5. **Next steps** (ten minutes): What decisions need to be made, by
   when, and by whom.

The meeting becomes a strategic discussion about what to do, not a
debate about what the findings mean.

The Pattern: Involvement Throughout Creates Ownership

Before research: Stakeholders shape questions → feel invested in
answers.

During research: Stakeholders see emerging themes → process gradually,
not defensively.

Mid-research: Stakeholders participate in synthesis → feel they
discovered insights.

Pre-presentation: Stakeholders preview findings → time to process
privately.

The presentation: Stakeholders confirm what they already know →
discussion about action, not debate about findings.

Involvement throughout creates ownership. Ownership drives action.

That's how research becomes impact instead of sitting in Confluence.

The strategic decision: Never surprise stakeholders
with research findings. Involve them before research
starts (shaping questions), during research (emerging
themes), mid-research (collaborative synthesis), and
before formal presentations (individual previews). By

the time you present formally, stakeholders should already know what you're going to say—the presentation becomes a strategic discussion about action, not a debate about whether findings are valid. This progressive involvement is the difference between research that sits in Confluence and research that drives product decisions.

Using Clips Strategically

Remember from Chapter 4 why clips matter: They're undeniable, build empathy, create shared understanding, and make problems concrete.

Here's exactly how to use them in practice.

During Synthesis: Pull Strategic Clips

As you interview, note moments worth capturing:

- 30–90 seconds showing a user struggling with a specific task
- Clear illustration of a pattern that multiple users experienced (not outliers)
- Emotional moments revealing frustration or confusion
- Concrete examples of workarounds users created

What makes a good clip:

- Short (30–90 seconds maximum)
- Focused on one insight
- Representative of a pattern (not unique to one person)
- Shows authentic struggle (not coached or contrived)

How to identify clip-worthy moments:

During live interviews, jot quick timestamps when users:

- Get visibly frustrated
- Abandon a task mid-flow
- Create workarounds
- Say something particularly striking ("I have no idea if that worked")
- Succeed unexpectedly (showing what DOES work well)

After each interview session, review your timestamps and pull 1-3 clips that illustrate emerging patterns.

In Presentations: 2–3 Clips Maximum

Don't overwhelm stakeholders with fifteen clips. Choose 2–3 that illustrate your most important insights.

Before each clip: Frame context: "Watch what happens when she tries to assign licenses."

Set up what to look for: "Notice how she checks three different screens trying to find what's already assigned."

During the clip: Let it play without interruption. Don't narrate over the user's struggle—let stakeholders experience it.

Ask: "What did you notice?" "What surprised you?" Let stakeholders voice their reactions.

After each clip:

Discuss implications: "This is why we need state visibility—without it, admins waste time hunting across multiple screens and still can't confirm what's assigned.

In Roadmap Discussions: Reference Specific Clips

When advocating for priorities weeks or months later, reference clips that stakeholders remember.

- "Remember that admin who spent twelve minutes trying to assign licenses and finally gave up? This addresses that exact moment."
- "Think back to that teacher who abandoned rostering at step three. Our solution eliminates the confusion she experienced."

Clips create a shared language for user problems that persists beyond the research phase. They're more memorable than written findings.

In Chapter 9, we'll cover how to strategically frame your findings and recommendations for different stakeholder types when advocating for prioritization—including how to use clips as part of your advocacy strategy.

Practical Considerations

Always get participant consent for sharing clips with internal teams. Include this in recruitment and consent forms: "We may share video/audio clips of this session with internal product and design teams. Your name and any identifying information will be kept confidential."

Keep clips short (30–90 seconds) and focused on specific moments. Long clips lose impact. If the struggle lasted eight minutes, excerpt the most illustrative sixty seconds.

Provide context before playing clips so stakeholders know what to watch for. "Watch what happens when she tries to create a differentiated assignment—notice where she gets stuck."

Select clips that show the pattern, not outliers. One frustrated user might be an anomaly. Similar struggles from three users? That's a pattern worth showing.

Balance negative and positive clips. Problems need fixing, but stakeholders also need to see what's working well. Show both to maintain credibility and morale.

Anonymize appropriately. If showing clips outside your immediate team, blur faces or use audio-only if the participant requested anonymity. Always honor privacy commitments.

Test clips before presentations. Make sure audio is clear, video quality is sufficient, and the clip starts and ends where you intended. Technical difficulties kill impact.

The strategic decision: Clips don't just support your insights—they make stakeholders *feel* the problem. And when stakeholders feel the problem, they're motivated to solve it.

Clips Can Change Everything

The most persuasive research isn't the most comprehensive. It's the research that makes the problem real for decision-makers.

Moving Forward to Design and Advocacy

You now understand strategic execution using your selected toolkit:

Fast-to-insight through strategic sampling (patterns often visible by interview five when participants are selected strategically), rolling synthesis (insights emerging during research, not weeks after), and parallel work (don't wait sequentially)

Signal vs. noise recognition (act on patterns repeated across three or more participants and confirmed by data, not individual preferences)

EdTech-specific execution (respect seasonal access, plan student research six months ahead, compensate teachers appropriately)

Progressive stakeholder involvement (input before research, emerging themes during, collaborative synthesis mid-way, individual previews before presentations, and confirmation, not revelation, in formal meetings)

Strategic clip usage (pull 30–90 second moments during synthesis, use 2–3 in presentations, reference in roadmap discussions, match to stakeholder concerns, and always get consent)

Tools selected. Research executed using those tools effectively. Insights generated. Stakeholders bought in.

Next question: How do we translate findings into designed solutions and advocate for their prioritization?

That's Phases 4 and 5: Develop strategy and advocate for direction, then design solutions and advocate for prioritization—covered in Chapters 9 and 10.

→ For execution templates, stakeholder communication scripts, synthesis frameworks, clip selection guides, and participant recruitment strategies, check out *The Strategic UX Toolkit Playbook* (available at kellymorganux.com).

PHASE 4

Develop Strategy and Advocate for Direction

"If you don't know where you are going, you'll end up someplace else." — ***Yogi Berra***

"If you don't know your UX Strategy, you'll end up building someone's feature request instead." — ***Yogi Berra (adapted)***

Research insights don't automatically become product changes.

Here's what I learned: Research becomes a strategic direction when you translate findings into a UX strategy that guides every design decision, then builds the case for why specific problems and opportunities deserve investment.

This is where research becomes strategy. Where insights become direction. And where user needs become organizational commitment to solving specific problems.

Phase 4 is the first major synthesis phase in your toolkit-building process. You've selected tools (Phase 2) and used them effectively (Phase 3). Now you're synthesizing what you learned into a strategic direction.

181

The UX Strategy

A UX Strategy isn't a tagline. It's not a marketing phrase. It's a decision filter that grounds every design choice you make—a tool that guides which other tools and approaches you'll use.

What is a UX Strategy?

A UX Strategy articulates how your product helps users solve their problems, often by thinking of the system as a type of agent working on the user's behalf.

It's developed by understanding:

- Users' perception of their problem
- What limits their ability to solve it on their own
- How the product could help bridge that gap

The best UX Strategies look at how users solve problems in the analog world and determine how the product can automate tasks or fill knowledge gaps to help them complete those tasks more effectively.

How Does a UX Strategy Help?

A UX Strategy operationalizes your product vision by providing a specific question to ask at each decision point:

Will this [design choice, feature, user flow, etc.] help achieve our strategy?

- When your team debates whether to build Feature A or Feature B, the UX Strategy provides the criteria.
- When you're deciding how to sequence a workflow, the UX Strategy guides the logic.

- When you're advocating for design direction, the UX Strategy gives you the "why" that connects user needs to product decisions.

Example of Strategy in Action

Let's say your EdTech product serves teachers who struggle to differentiate instruction for diverse learners. Your UX Strategy might be: "Act as a personalized instructional assistant that automates lesson differentiation based on student data."

Now, when deciding features:

- "Should we build a content library or an AI-powered differentiation engine?" → Strategy says: differentiation engine (fills the knowledge gap about what each student needs).
- "Should we surface all student data or provide actionable recommendations?" → Strategy says: recommendations (reduces cognitive load, acts as an assistant).
- "Should we make bulk operations easy or focus on individual student customization?" → Strategy says: both, but prioritize individual customization (matches the strategy of personalization).

Without a strategy, these become opinion debates. With a strategy, they become strategic decisions grounded in how you've committed to helping users.

When You'll Develop Your Strategy

You don't create a UX Strategy before research—you develop it from research insights and adjust it over time as your product, market, and insights evolve.

In Phase 1 (Chapter 6), you'll assess your context. In Phase 2 (Chapter 7), you'll select research tools. In Phase 3 (Chapter 8), you'll execute research and build stakeholder buy-in.

Then in Phase 4 (Chapter 9), you'll synthesize those insights into a UX Strategy that guides design decisions and advocacy. The strategy becomes the foundation for which design tools you'll use and how you'll advocate for what users need.

Think of your UX Strategy as the North Star tool that emerges from understanding users deeply—it's what makes your design decisions strategic rather than reactive.

From Findings to Strategic Interpretation

Research generates insights. But raw insights aren't enough—you need to interpret what they mean strategically before you can develop a UX Strategy or advocate for which problems to pursue.

This interpretation phase answers four critical questions:

1. What problems did research uncover?

Not "users said they want X feature." But "users struggling to accomplish Y task because a Z workflow gap exists."

The difference matters. Features are solutions users imagined. Problems are obstacles blocking outcomes.

2. What outcomes do users actually need?

Remember Principle 3 (Chapter 4): outcomes over features.

When a teacher says "I need bulk grading," they're not describing their actual need. They're proposing a solution.

So, what's the outcome they need? It might be "Give meaningful feedback on 150 assignments in under two hours instead of spending my entire weekend grading" or something else.

That outcome might require bulk operations. Or it might require intelligent defaults, keyboard shortcuts, saved feedback templates, or AI-assisted draft responses. Or probably some combination.

You can't know until you design for the outcome, not the requested feature.

At one company, a single feature request—"bring back the direct-assignment feature"—actually represented seven different user needs. These ranged from distrust of the algorithm that recommended skills to wanting students to work in small groups and needing a way to direct them to the appropriate shared skills.

3. What's the user's knowledge gap?

This is where strategic interpretation gets powerful.

For every task users struggle with, there's a knowledge gap:

- **User knowledge:** What does the user know when approaching this task?
- **Task knowledge:** What knowledge is required to complete the task successfully?
- **Knowledge gap:** The difference between what users know and what they need to know.

Understanding the knowledge gap tells you how your product can help.

Example: Teachers want to divide students into small groups, with each group working on skills all members need.

- **User knowledge:** The teacher knows their students' general strengths and weaknesses.
- **Task knowledge:** Identifying which skills each student needs for the unit and how to best group students so they're working on common skills gaps.
- **Knowledge gap:** The specific skills each student lacks and how to form groups with maximum overlap in skill needs.

Product's role: Fill the knowledge gap by:

- Suggesting groups of students based on the teacher's unit goal and group size preferences
- Allowing for manual updates to accommodate contexts that the product doesn't have (students who don't work well together, etc.)
- Suggesting updates based on manual changes (to balance groups if students are moved, or suggest another possible move that better overlaps skill needs of group members)

The knowledge gap framework helps you design systems that fill in what users don't know as they work through unfamiliar tasks.

This approach—focusing on knowledge gaps rather than user personas— is brilliantly detailed in *Disruptive Research* by Larry Marine and Debbie Levitt. I'm a big fan of this knowledge-oriented approach because it centers design on what users actually need to know to be successful, not demographic details that rarely inform effective design decisions.

4. What's feasible given constraints?

Your research might reveal that teachers need something radically different. But if implementing it requires rebuilding core platform architecture, and you have fifteen years of technical debt and only six months until launch, that "perfect" solution isn't feasible.

Remember your context assessment from Chapter 6: Recommendations must align with organizational maturity, roadmap flexibility, and technical reality.

The strategic decision: Feasibility isn't optional. Research within your constraints, or come prepared to advocate for the resources needed to change them— with phasing plans, cost estimates, and user research data to back your case.

Developing Your UX Strategy

Now that you understand the problems, outcomes, and knowledge gaps, you're ready to develop your UX Strategy: the decision filter that will guide every design choice going forward.

What Makes a Strong UX Strategy

A UX Strategy isn't a feature list. It's not a roadmap. It's a statement of how your product helps users solve their problems.

Strong UX Strategies share three characteristics:

1. Grounded in user problems, not product features

Weak: "Provide comprehensive reporting dashboards."

Strong: "Act as a data interpreter that translates raw student performance into actionable instructional decisions."

The strong version describes the role your product plays in users' work— it fills the knowledge gap between raw data and actionable insights.

2. Operationalizable as a decision filter

Your strategy should provide a specific question to ask at each design decision:

"Will this [feature/flow/choice] help us [fulfill our strategy]?"

If you can't use your strategy to decide between two design directions, it's not operational enough.

3. Describes the product as an agent working on the users' behalf

The best strategies frame the product as a collaborator or assistant, something that extends the user's capabilities.

- "Digital instructional coach" > "Content management system"
- "Automated differentiation assistant" > "Lesson planning tool"
- "Administrative workflow partner" > "District management platform"

This framing helps you design proactively (what would a good assistant do?) rather than reactively (what features do users request?).

How to Develop Your Strategy

<u>Step 1: Understand users' perception of their problem</u>

What's blocking them from success? Not "What features are they missing?" but "What are they trying to accomplish that's currently too hard, too time-consuming, or requires knowledge they don't have?"

From your research in Phase 3 (Chapter 8), synthesize:

- Common struggles across users
- Workarounds they've created
- Tasks they avoid because they're too difficult
- Knowledge gaps that create friction

<u>Step 2: Identify how the problem is solved in the analog world</u>

How do successful users accomplish this without technology? Or with competitors? Or with manual processes? Or with your product and the workarounds or task aids they created to use?

This reveals the task structure and knowledge requirements. Understanding the analog workflow shows you what's essential (must be preserved in your product) versus what's a limitation (should be automated away).

<u>Step 3: Articulate how your product bridges the gap</u>

Given the problem and the analog solution, what role should your product play?

Should it:

- Automate manual tasks?

- Fill knowledge gaps?
- Reduce cognitive load?
- Provide expertise that users lack?
- Enable collaboration?
- Surface patterns humans miss?

Your strategy should clearly articulate this role.

Strategy Example: The Digital Instructional Coach

Let me show you how this works in practice:

<u>Users' perception of their problem:</u>

Teachers don't have the time or knowledge to:

- Customize pre-defined lesson sequences to fit their specific classroom needs
- Parse through content libraries to ensure vertical and horizontal alignment
- Analyze student data and understand the "what now" that would help each learner
- Find relevant resources to upskill their own pedagogical knowledge
- Incorporate yet another technology tool into their already overwhelmed workflow

<u>How this problem is solved in the analog world:</u>

Some districts employ Instructional Technology Coaches (ITCs) who:

- Help teachers integrate technology effectively
- Design professional development on digital tools

- Ensure technology aligns with curriculum standards
- Find and curate appropriate digital resources
- Collaborate with teachers to develop a shared vision
- Analyze data to inform instructional improvements
- Model best practices and demonstrate effective integration

Not all districts can afford ITCs, which means many teachers have no one to fill this knowledge gap.

Product strategy:

Act as a digital instructional technology coach that automates routine differentiation, curates aligned content, interprets student data into actionable next steps, and provides just-in-time pedagogical guidance—extending what ITCs do for teachers who have them, and filling that gap for teachers who don't.

How this operationalizes:

Every design decision gets filtered through: "Will this help teachers feel like they're working with a knowledgeable instructional coach?"

- **Feature request**: "Teachers want a content library" → Strategy says: Don't just provide library access, curate relevant content based on what they're teaching and recommend specific resources for specific student needs (like a coach would).
- **Design decision**: "Should we surface all student data?" → Strategy says: No, interpret the data and provide coaching recommendations like "three students struggling with data manipulation—here are targeted interventions" (like a coach would).

- **Workflow question**: "Where should differentiation settings live?" → Strategy says: In a context where teachers are assigning work, with smart suggestions based on student data (like a coach would offer guidance at the moment of planning).

The strategy transforms opinion debates into strategic decisions grounded in the role you've committed to playing in users' work.

Testing Your Strategy

Before you commit to a UX Strategy, validate it:

<u>Does it resonate with users?</u>

Describe the strategy (not features) to a few users: "Imagine a product that acts as your digital instructional coach—analyzing student data, suggesting interventions, curating resources ..."

Do they light up? "That's exactly what I need!"

Or do they seem confused? "So ... it's a content library?"

If users can't envision how the strategy would help them, refine it.

<u>Does it differentiate from competitors?</u>

Many EdTech products are "learning management systems" or "assessment platforms." If your strategy sounds like every competitor's, it won't guide distinctive design decisions.

<u>Can it drive design decisions?</u>

Test it against real decisions you're facing. Does the strategy provide clear direction? Or could you justify both options equally well?

If the strategy doesn't help you choose between competing priorities, it's not operational enough.

<u>Does it align with business goals?</u>

Your strategy must serve both users and business objectives. If the strategy requires capabilities your business can't support or contradicts revenue models, it won't survive organizational reality.

Once validated, your UX Strategy becomes the foundation for advocacy and design.

The strategic decision: A strategy you can't use to make decisions isn't a strategy—it's a tagline. Test yours against real design choices before committing to it.

Advocating for Research Insights and Strategic Opportunities

You now understand the problems, outcomes, and knowledge gaps, and have developed a UX Strategy. Before you design specific solutions, you need to advocate for why these problems matter and why your strategy is the right approach.

This is the first wave of advocacy: building buy-in for the direction before investing in detailed design work.

Framing Problems for Different Stakeholders

The same research insights need different framing based on what each stakeholder cares about.

For executives: Connect to business impact

Start with how user problems translate to business risk.

"Teachers abandon rostering after fifteen minutes → 30 percent incomplete setups at school start → impacts data quality for all reporting → threatens district renewals."

Not: "Teachers find rostering confusing."

Connect user problems to strategic goals. If the company's focus is market expansion, frame it as competitive positioning: "Competitors fail at differentiation. We can win districts by solving what others ignore."

For product managers: Clarify opportunity size

PMs need to understand impact vs. effort at the problem level, not just the solution level.

"Admin license assignment problems affect 100 percent of district admins. This happens three times a year at critical moments, generates 25 percent of our support volume, and correlates with renewal risk."

Not: "Admins struggle with licenses."

Help them see the opportunity before asking them to commit to the roadmap space.

<u>For engineers: Show the technical problem space</u>

Engineers want to understand the problem before discussing solutions.

"Teachers create workarounds because our system doesn't preserve draft state, so they've learned not to trust that partial work saves."

Not: "We should add autosave."

When engineers understand the user problem (trust issues from lost work), they can suggest technical approaches you might not have considered.

<u>For designers: Connect to user goals</u>

Designers want to understand user mental models and workflow context.

"Teachers expect assignment creation to work like their LMS: linear, preview-focused, edit-anytime. Our system assumes they plan completely before creating, which breaks their flow."

Not: "The UI is confusing."

Framing helps designers see the mental model mismatch, not just surface usability issues.

Presenting Your UX Strategy

Once stakeholders understand the problems, present your strategy as the guiding principle for solutions.

<u>Structure for strategy presentation:</u>

1. **Remind them of the problems** (five minutes): "Here's what we learned about teacher struggles ..."

2. **Show the analog solution** (five minutes): "Here's how successful teachers solve this now with ITCs ..."
3. **Present the strategy** (ten minutes): "Our strategy is to act as a digital instructional technology coach that ..."
4. **Demonstrate decision-making power** (fifteen minutes): Walk through 2–3 recent decisions and show how the strategy would have guided them differently. Use real debates they remember.
5. **Get commitment** (ten minutes): "Does this strategy resonate? Do you see how it guides design? Are there concerns we should address?"

The goal isn't just buy-in on the strategy—it's a shared understanding that this strategy will be the filter for design decisions going forward.

Advocacy Calibrated to UX Maturity

Remember from Chapter 6: Your organization's UX maturity determines what they're ready to hear and believe.

Ad-hoc maturity organizations:

- **What they'll believe:** Concrete problems with measurable costs.
- **What they won't believe yet:** Strategic vision, long-term thinking.
- **Your advocacy approach:** Focus on specific problems with business impact, show quick wins that prove UX value.
- **Hold back:** Big strategic vision conversations—they need proof before strategy.

Defined maturity organizations:

- **What they'll believe:** Research-backed problems, user needs driving decisions.

- **What they won't believe yet:** User needs should override business requirements.
- **Your advocacy approach:** Frame problems with research evidence, connect to strategic goals, and show how UX strategy aligns with business strategy.
- **Hold back:** Delay pushing back too hard on business constraints. They need to see UX as a partner, not an adversary.

Managed/Optimizing maturity organizations:

- **What they'll believe:** Strategic UX thinking, long-term vision.
- **What they value:** UX influence on business strategy, not just product features.
- **Your advocacy approach:** Lead with strategy, use research as validation, and propose category-defining innovations.
- **Opportunity:** UX strategy can shape business strategy.

Calibrating your advocacy to their maturity level determines whether stakeholders see you as a credible strategic partner or an idealistic designer who doesn't understand business reality.

Moving Forward to Design

You now understand Phase 4 of the Strategic UX Toolkit: How to interpret research findings strategically, develop a UX Strategy that guides decisions, and advocate for directional alignment before investing in design work.

Strategic interpretation answered four questions:

- What problems did research uncover?
- What outcomes do users actually need?
- What's the user's knowledge gap?

- What's feasible given constraints?

UX Strategy development created a decision filter that:

- is grounded in user problems, not product features.
- is operationalizable at each decision point.
- frames the product as an agent working on the users' behalf.

Directional advocacy built buy-in:

- Framed problems for different stakeholders
- Presented strategy with decision-making examples
- Calibrated approach to organizational maturity

Now your stakeholders are aligned on which problems to solve and how your product should help. You have a UX Strategy that will guide every design decision—a critical tool in your toolkit.

Next: "How do we translate strategy into designed solutions and get them prioritized and shipped?"

That's Phase 5: Design solutions and strategic advocacy—covered in Chapter 10.

→ For strategy development templates, stakeholder presentation frameworks, and problem framing tools, check out *The Strategic UX Toolkit Playbook* (available at kellymorganux.com).

PHASE 5

Design Solutions and Advocate for Prioritization

*"Perfect is the enemy of good." — **Voltaire***

*"Perfect is the enemy of shipped, but good enough is the enemy of user trust in EdTech's nine-month lock-in." — **Voltaire (adapted)***

You've developed your UX Strategy. You've secured stakeholder alignment on which problems to solve and how your product should help users. Now comes the final phase of toolkit-building: Translating that strategic direction into designed solutions, then building the case for why those specific solutions should be prioritized and shipped. This is where strategy becomes design. Where direction becomes workflows. And where organizational commitment becomes shipped features that users actually experience.

Phase 5 completes your toolkit by adding design and implementation advocacy tools.

Setting Up Designers to Design Effectively

When working with other designers, frame information around craft and system thinking.

- **Show how recommended solutions align with established patterns**: "This extends the pattern we use in the gradebook to the assignment flow."
- **Highlight component reusability**: "Use existing design system elements to maintain consistency."
- **Emphasize accessibility from the start**: "WCAG 2.2 AA compliance is built in, not retrofitted."
- **Connect to design principles**: "Reduces cognitive load through progressive disclosure, which is a core principle in our system."

When using clips with designers: Show clips revealing interaction and workflow problems.

- User is expecting different behavior from the interface element
- User is lost in navigation
- User is repeatedly clicking the wrong thing (mental model mismatch)

Designers need to understand how users mentally model the interface and where those models break down. Clips showing users with the wrong expectations help designers see where the design isn't communicating effectively. Clips showing navigation confusion point to information architecture problems.

The strategic decision: Designers solve problems they can see. Frame research around craft and systems—show where user mental models break from interface expectations, and designers will know exactly what to fix.

Knowledge Profiles vs. User Personas

User personas are often used in the design processes. They're intended to humanize the process and help designers focus on users and their needs. Personas can get elaborate with fictional names, demographics, quotes, life goals, etc. Many teams spend significant time distilling research into these fictional user personas—then never actually use them during design.

Most information in user personas isn't especially helpful to design. They become hyper-specific ("a single mother in her thirties who is an avid reader and loves the outdoors") with details that won't help you design for their actual needs.

Knowledge-oriented design takes a different approach. Rather than focusing on users by creating hyper-specific fictional characters, it centers design on users' different knowledge profiles:

- **User knowledge:** What knowledge is the user bringing into the situation?
- **Task knowledge:** What knowledge is needed to complete the task?
- **Knowledge gap:** The gap between the user's knowledge and the knowledge required to complete the task.

When a product fills the knowledge gap and mirrors how successful users naturally complete the task, it becomes truly effective.

Why knowledge profiles are more useful than personas:

Personas: "Meet Sarah, a 35-year-old fifth-grade teacher with eight years of experience who loves hiking..."

Knowledge profile: "Experienced teacher segment: Knows pedagogy and classroom management, lacks knowledge of platform data architecture and how assignments connect to reporting, needs the system to fill this gap by explaining the implications of choices at decision points."

The persona tells you about Sarah as a person. The knowledge profile tells you exactly what your product needs to provide to help teachers like Sarah succeed.

Knowledge profiles keep design conversations focused on: "What does this user know? What do they need to know? How do we fill that gap?" These questions directly drive design decisions.

The strategic decision: Personas are usually meant to "humanize" the user for stakeholders. Use clips for that and knowledge profiles for design work.

Task-Based Design Thinking

Your UX Strategy provides the "why" behind your product. Now you need to design the "how"—the actual workflows that enable users to achieve their goals.

Here's the shift that transforms how you design for EdTech: Design complete workflows that enable outcomes, not disconnected features.

Let me explain with an analogy from my teaching days.

The Science Lab Equipment Analogy

When setting up a science classroom, I've seen two ways to handle lab equipment.

Equipment-by-drawer approach: Each lab table has a drawer assigned to a class period. That drawer contains standard equipment—beakers in various sizes, test tubes, graduated cylinders, stirring rods, thermometers, and everything students might need all year.

That works great for accountability. You know exactly which period broke the 250mL beaker because it's assigned to that class's drawer.

But it's terrible for student learning. When lab instructions say "get a heat-resistant container," students are staring at their drawer full of glassware, wondering: Is that a beaker or a flask? Which size? Do I need the one with the pour spout? They're spending cognitive energy on equipment identification instead of understanding the experiment.

Task-based lab kits: I kept all equipment in the back room and set out a tub at each lab table with exactly what students needed for that day's experiment. The "titration lab" tub had the right size beaker, the correct burette, the specific indicator solution, the volumetric flask, and the pipette—everything matching the procedure.

Students grabbed the tub and started working. No hunting through drawers. No matching equipment names to unfamiliar glassware. They learned equipment names faster because they only had the items that matched the instructions.

As the expert, I could efficiently pull from organized back-room storage (all beakers together, all graduated cylinders together) because I knew the equipment taxonomy. But I gave students—the novices—a kit organized around their task, not around equipment categories.

That meant a lower cognitive load for students, faster setup, and better learning outcomes. The organization matched how students think about the task ("I'm doing a titration"), not how equipment experts categorize tools.

Applied to EdTech Products

Feature-oriented products scatter capabilities across the interface. Search functionality here. Filtering there. Bulk actions somewhere else. Export to another section.

Users must figure out which features they need for their task, then hunt for them across the product. This requires product expertise—understanding the feature set and where everything lives.

Task-oriented products organize workflows around tasks users actually do. "Assign licenses before school starts" has everything needed in logical sequence—who needs licenses, what's available, bulk assignment, progress visibility, error prevention, and confirmation.

Users follow the workflow and accomplish their goal. Product expertise is not required.

Why This Matters in EdTech

Remember from Chapter 2: Teachers are time-poor and cognitively overloaded. They can't afford to learn complex feature sets. They need to accomplish tasks quickly within their existing workflow.

Feature-oriented design adds cognitive load: "Which features do I need? Where are they? And in what order?" This is especially true for features that only fit in their workflow a few times a year (like rostering). By the time they need them again, it's been **6-12** months, and they've forgotten.

Task-based design reduces cognitive load: "Here's the path to your goal. Follow these steps."

That difference determines adoption.

A Note on Clicks and Confidence

There's a common misconception that good UX means "reducing clicks" or "removing friction." That's oversimplified and often wrong. Good task-based design ensures each click is made with confidence that it's moving the user closer to their goal, and each friction point is intentional and matches the user's mental model. Sometimes this means MORE steps, not fewer.

Example: License assignment

Feature-based (fewer clicks, low confidence):

1. Select all teachers
2. Bulk assign licenses
3. Submit

Fast? Yes. Confident? No. Users have no idea what just happened, whether they assigned the right licenses, or if they made a mistake, until it's too late.

Task-based (more clicks, high confidence):

1. Review who needs licenses (clear visibility).

2. See what's available and already assigned (system remembers context).
3. Select teachers with smart defaults (system suggests based on patterns).
4. Preview what will happen when you submit (system fills knowledge gap).
5. Confirm assignments (clear outcome state).

While this involves more steps, each step provides information that increases confidence. Users know what they're doing at each point. They can catch mistakes before they happen and understand what was accomplished when they're done.

The strategic decision: It's not about reducing clicks and friction—it's about strategically revealing options based on task context and ensuring users feel confident at each step.

Task-based design sometimes means showing less (because not everything needs to be visible all the time), sometimes means showing more (because users need confidence-building information), and always means matching the interface to how users think about the task, not how engineers organized the features.

For a comprehensive exploration of task-based design, mapping workflows and knowledge profiles, see *Disruptive Research* by Larry Marine and Debbie Levitt. They provide detailed frameworks for mapping task structures and identifying knowledge gaps that your product can fill.

Account for All Three Users When Mapping Task Flows

In addition to the process described by Marine and Levitt, remember from Chapter 2: EdTech often involves three users in the workflow chain.

You can't optimize one step at the expense of others:

Easy assignment creation (teacher) BUT hard to find (student) = fails

- Teachers think it's assigned.
- Students can't find it.
- Learning doesn't happen.

Beautiful student experience, BUT confusing teacher setup = never gets used

- Brilliant content that teachers won't assign because creation is painful
- Students never see the great experience

Efficient admin reporting, BUT requires extra teacher data entry = low adoption

- Teachers abandon products that create administrative overhead.
- Efficiency for one user type shouldn't create work for another.

The strategic consideration: Who controls adoption?

Usually it's the teacher. Their workflow is make-or-break. Student workflow matters for retention and learning outcomes. Admin workflow matters for renewals and compliance. But if teachers don't adopt, none of the rest matters.

Design Communication Artifacts

Design isn't just final mockups. It's a progression from exploring possibilities to validating specific solutions, using different communication tools at different stages to communicate with stakeholders and test with users.

These artifacts are tools in your toolkit for communicating design decisions and building stakeholder confidence in your solutions.

User Flows: Mapping Task Logic

User flows document the complete path users take through a workflow—including decision points, error states, and alternative paths.

When to create user flows:

- Early in design, before detailed mockups
- When workflow logic is complex with multiple paths
- To communicate with engineers about required system states
- To validate the task structure with stakeholders before visual design

What makes a good user flow:

- Shows all paths, not just the happy path (what happens when users make mistakes, encounter errors, or take alternative routes?)
- Identifies decision points clearly (what choices must users make, what information do they need to choose wisely?)
- Includes system state (what does the system remember, what carries forward to the next step?)

User flows help you validate that the workflow logic makes sense before investing in visual design. They're also powerful advocacy tools.

Stakeholders can see the complete scope of a feature before development begins.

Storyboards: Visualizing Context

Storyboards show how your product fits into users' actual work context—not just the interface, but the environment and situation in which they're using it.

When to create storyboards:

- To communicate why specific design choices matter, given real-world constraints
- To help stakeholders understand the user context that they don't experience directly
- To validate that your design accounts for classroom/district realities

What makes a good storyboard:

- Shows the trigger (what prompts the user to use this feature?)
- Illustrates environmental constraints (using this in a classroom with thirty students, not in a quiet office)
- Depicts the complete task (not just product interaction, but before and after)
- Reveals emotional state (frustration, confidence, anxiety)

Storyboards build empathy with stakeholders who don't directly experience the user context.

Usability Testing as Validation and Advocacy

Usability testing isn't just for finding problems—it's proof that your design works (or needs iteration) before you commit development resources.

Strategic usability testing:

- **Test early** with low-fidelity prototypes (paper sketches, wireframes) to validate workflow logic before visual design.
- **Test iteratively** as design progresses (validate improvements, don't wait for "done").
- **Test with realistic tasks** in realistic contexts (not "explore the interface" but "roster your students before school starts").

Usability testing as an advocacy tool:

Testing results provide proof for design decisions:

"We tested the two-step workflow with six teachers. Five of six completed successfully in under five minutes. When we tested the previous four-step workflow, only two of six completed successfully, and it took over twelve minutes. The simpler workflow isn't just 'better UX'—it's the difference between successful adoption and frustrated abandonment."

Quantitative usability metrics (task completion rates, time on task, error rates) translate design improvements into business language. Qualitative insights (user quotes, moments of confusion, unexpected successes) provide the human story.

The combination is powerful advocacy: Stakeholders see both the data (this design works measurably better) and the user experience (watch this teacher succeed easily).

The strategic decision: Test before building. In EdTech's high lock-in context, you don't have the luxury of launching minimally viable and iterating based on user feedback. Usability testing lets you iterate before launch, when changes are cheap.

Design for EdTech-Specific Constraints

Beyond general task-based thinking, EdTech has specific constraints that should inform every design decision.

Accessibility as a Strategic Advantage

Let me be direct: accessibility isn't a checkbox exercise. It's a competitive differentiator and design philosophy that improves your product for everyone.

The compliance mindset: "We need to meet WCAG 2.2 AA so we can get approved."

This leads to retrofitting accessibility after design, treating it as a burden, and doing the minimum necessary.

The strategic mindset: "Accessible design is better design for ALL users, and accessibility is more than WCAG (like mental models, reducing extraneous cognitive load, task-flow design, etc.)."

This leads to building accessibility into your design system from the start, seeing it as a design principle, and exceeding minimum requirements.

Why the strategic mindset matters:

- **Color contrast** helps users in bright classrooms with glare on screens, not just users with visual impairments, but every teacher dealing with sunlight through windows or old projectors washing out displays.
- **Clear visual hierarchy** reduces cognitive load for overwhelmed teachers, not just screen reader users. Every teacher scanning quickly between classes benefits from knowing what's most important at a glance.
- **Keyboard navigation** enables efficiency for power users, not just users who can't use mice, but teachers who've learned keyboard shortcuts accomplish tasks faster.
- **Simple language** benefits English language learners, not just users with cognitive disabilities, but students and teachers for whom English isn't their first language, or anyone reading quickly under time pressure.
- **Consistent patterns** reduce the learning curve across the product, not just users with cognitive disabilities, but every user benefits from predictable interaction patterns.

I always advocate for building accessibility into the design system from day one.

The benefit? Every new feature is automatically accessible. Designers don't have to retrofit—it's built into the components they're using.

This becomes a competitive advantage. Many EdTech products fail accessibility audits, but products with foundational accessibility pass without special effort. The strategic investment pays dividends across the entire product.

Designing for Cognitive Load

Remember from Chapter 2: Teachers manage 150 students across multiple classes while juggling administrative demands, parent communication, and actual teaching. Their cognitive capacity is maxed out before they even open your product.

Your interface can't add to that cognitive load—it must reduce it.

Progressive disclosure: Show essential information first and details on demand. Don't overwhelm users with everything at once. Surface what they need to know immediately. Make additional details available when needed.

Smart defaults: Reduce the decisions users must make. Every decision point adds cognitive load. Where can the product make intelligent choices based on context or patterns? This isn't about removing control—it's about removing unnecessary cognitive work. Users can still make different choices when needed.

Visual hierarchy for skimmability: Make the most important information prominent. Teachers scan quickly; they don't read carefully. Can they accomplish their task by reading headers and key information without processing every word? Or do they need to read in-product instructions, descriptions, and help text to figure out how to use a feature? Size, color, position, contrast—all communicate importance. Use them intentionally.

Consistent patterns: The same action should always be in the same place and in the same format. Users shouldn't have to relearn patterns in different sections of your product. If "Edit" is a pencil icon in one section, it should be a pencil icon everywhere. If confirming actions requires clicking "Save" in one workflow, don't make it "Submit" or "Continue" in another. Consistency here reduces cognitive load significantly—users build muscle memory instead of having to think about interface mechanics.

The strategic decision: Teachers arrive cognitively maxed out. Design every screen assuming users have no spare mental capacity—because they don't.

Designing for a Wide Range of Savviness

EdTech users are vastly different:

- Teachers who avoid technology and teachers who code in their free time
- Five-year-old students and eighteen-year-old students
- First-year teachers and thirty-year veterans

You can't design only for novices because you'll frustrate experts. And you can't design only for experts because you'll alienate novices.

Scaffolding: Help novices without slowing experts

Here are a few ways to achieve that balance. Provide:

- Support for new users that experienced users can skip or ignore
- Onboarding tutorials that are skippable for returning users
- Contextual help that's available but not forced
- Tool tips that appear once and can be dismissed

Multiple paths to the same outcome

- **Novice path:** Offer a step-by-step wizard with explanations at each stage.
- **Expert path:** Give direct access to all controls, keyboard shortcuts, and bulk operations.

Both paths accomplish the same goal. Users choose based on their comfort level.

I learned this from my high school teaching days. Forcing everyone down the same path frustrated half the class. Some students needed structured step-by-step instructions. Others wanted the problem and the freedom to solve it their way. Both approaches led to learning.

The same principle applies to product design.

Progressive complexity: The core functionality is simple, and advanced features are available but not primary.

The strategic decision: The default experience should work well out of the box. Novices accomplish their goals without configuration or lots of training and documentation. But power users can access advanced features and customization when ready. They're not hidden—they're just not in the primary workflow.

Design Systems as Strategic Assets

A design system is a library of reusable components with usage guidelines. Buttons, form inputs, cards, modals, navigation patterns—all documented, coded, and accessible.

Why this matters strategically:

- **Creates consistency:** Users learn patterns once, and then apply them everywhere. It reduces cognitive load across the product.
- **Reduces development time:** Designers prototype faster using proven components. Engineers build faster using coded, tested components.
- **Enables faster iteration:** Test patterns once and use them in many places. Usability improvements scale across the product. Accessibility built into components benefits the entire product immediately.

When to invest in design systems:

- **Early if:** You build a product from scratch, have design resources, and plan multiple features using shared patterns.
- **Later if:** You have an established product with inconsistent patterns. Gradually retrofit and document as you standardize.

The strategic decision: Invest once, benefit everywhere.

Advocating for Design Prioritization

You've developed your UX strategy and have secured buy-in for it (Phase 4). You've designed solutions grounded in task-based workflows. You've validated designs through usability testing.

Now comes the second wave of advocacy: getting your specific designed solutions prioritized and shipped.

Many well-researched, beautifully-designed solutions die here—in prioritization discussions where the user needs to compete against technical debt, business requirements, and stakeholder opinions.

Strategic advocacy translates designed solutions into stakeholder language.

Framing Designed Solutions by Stakeholder Type

Same designed solution, different framing based on what each stakeholder cares about.

<u>For executives: Business outcomes</u>

- **Start with business impact, not design improvements**. "This workflow redesign increases successful rostering completion by 18 percent → improves data quality for reporting → reduces district frustration that threatens renewals → estimated $500K retention impact." Not: "We made rostering more intuitive."
- **Connect to strategic goals**. If Q3 focus is expanding into new markets, frame as competitive positioning: "Competitor weakness we can exploit—they fail at this workflow, we'll excel."
- **Frame as investment with return**. "$20K research investment prevented $200K building the wrong solution. $40K development investment returns $500K retention value."

When using clips with executives: Show clips demonstrating business impact.

- User saying, "We might not renew if this doesn't improve."
- Admin abandoning the task after fifteen minutes of struggle.
- Teacher explaining why they stopped using a feature.

Executives need to understand that user problems translate to business risk. Clips that show users at the breaking point—considering churn, abandoning workflows, or articulating frustration—make the business case visceral.

<u>For product managers: Prioritization frameworks</u>

PMs live in trade-off land. Help them make informed decisions.

- **Make impact vs. effort explicit**: "High impact affecting 60 percent of users, ships in one sprint vs. medium impact affecting 20 percent of users, requires two months" or "This option only takes one sprint but will only benefit 20 percent of users, while this one requires two months but will impact 80 percent of users" (because the quickest solution isn't necessarily the best if it's impact won't be wide-spread!).
- **Show feature adoption implications**: "This workflow increases daily active usage 40 percent, which affects your engagement metrics."
- **Clarify roadmap trade-offs:** "If we do X, Y gets delayed to Q3—here's why that's the right call."

Provide clear recommendations with rationale, not just present options.

When using clips with PMs: Show clips revealing user value vs. cost to solve.

- User struggling with a high-frequency task (high value to fix)
- User finding a workaround that suggests the direction of a solution
- User succeeding easily with something they expected to be hard (shows what's working)

PMs need to understand the magnitude and frequency of problems. Clips showing daily struggles help them prioritize high-impact fixes. Clips showing successful workarounds can inspire lower-cost solutions.

<u>For engineers: Technical feasibility and respect</u>

Engineers are allergic to recommendations that ignore technical reality. Build credibility by understanding constraints.

- **Acknowledge implementation complexity**: "I know this is a two-month effort versus a two-week effort based on our architecture discussions, but here's why it's better in the long run for the product."
- **Show how recommendations fit within system**: "This uses existing design system patterns, so no new components are needed."
- **Respect their expertise**: Ask "What's technically feasible given our constraints?" Don't tell them to "build this exact thing."

When using clips with engineers: Show clips revealing technical vs. UX problems

- User confused by interface design (UX problem they can help solve)
- User reporting error messages or broken functionality (technical problem they own)
- User creating a manual workaround for missing automation (shows what to build)

Engineers need to understand whether the problem is in their code or in the design. Present clips that clearly show:

- Users confused by layout or interaction patterns to help engineers see UX problems
- Technical errors to help them prioritize bug fixes
- Workarounds will inspire automation opportunities

Building the Strategic Business Case

Stakeholders need to understand not just what users need, but why investing in those needs makes business sense.

Metrics that matter to business:

- **Retention:** Users who stayed versus churned, tied to specific improvements
- **Efficiency:** Time-on-task before/after, tasks completed faster
- **Support costs:** Ticket volume reduction, common issues resolved by design
- **Adoption:** Feature utilization rates, onboarding completion, engagement metrics
- **Satisfaction:** NPS changes, sentiment shifts in qualitative feedback

Translating to dollar impact:

You don't need to fabricate numbers. But you do need to translate UX improvements into business language that executives understand. Work with Product Managers and Support teams for help with numbers!

Retention improvement:

- Customer retention rate increase x lifetime value (LTV) = revenue impact

- Example calculation method: 5 percent retention increase × $50K average customer value × 200 customers = $500K revenue retained

Efficiency gains:

- User time saved × value of user time × number of users = value delivered
- Example calculation method: 15 minutes per day saved × 10,000 teachers × 180 school days × $30/hour teacher value = $13.5M annual value delivered to customers

Support cost reduction:

- Support hours saved × hourly cost = cost avoided
- Example calculation method: 200 support tickets monthly × 30 minutes average × $40/hour = $4K monthly savings = $48K annual

---

The strategic decision: Don't just prove user value—translate it. Retention rates, efficiency gains, and support cost reductions are how executives measure whether your work deserves resources.

Strategic Release Timing

Remember from Chapter 1: EdTech's adoption windows and lock-in periods dictate when changes can ship.

Big releases before school starts (June-August):

- Teachers have time to learn new workflows.

- You can provide training when they're receptive.
- Users expect changes at school year boundaries.

Small iterations mid-year:

- Bug fixes that don't change workflows
- Minor improvements users barely notice
- Performance optimizations

Hold disruptive changes:

- Even if development completes in February, strategic timing might mean waiting until July.
- Teachers can't absorb workflow changes mid-year when they're overwhelmed.
- Frame it as a business decision protecting your investment: "Shipping now wastes the work because adoption will suffer."

Using timing strategically in advocacy:

When stakeholders push to ship features immediately because they're "done," reference EdTech constraints you established in Part 1.

"Development is complete in March, but launching mid-year means teachers encounter this during their busiest period. They won't have the capacity to learn the new workflow, adoption will be poor, and we'll get negative feedback that could have been avoided. Waiting until July means teachers have summer professional development time to learn the system, and they expect changes at school year boundaries. Strategic timing protects our development investment by ensuring strong adoption."

This frames holding the release as a strategic business decision, not an unnecessary delay.

The strategic decision: "Done" doesn't mean "ship now." In EdTech, releasing at the wrong time wastes your development investment—strategic timing ensures the work actually gets adopted.

Measuring Impact and Closing the Loop

The work isn't done when the product ships. Strategic UX practitioners measure impact and close the loop with stakeholders.

Track Metrics Defined Pre-Launch

Before shipping, establish baseline metrics. After shipping, track the same metrics to measure impact.

- **Before/after comparison:** Document baseline before changes, and measure the same metrics after launch.
- **Control for confounds:** What else changed simultaneously? Are you measuring the right thing?
- **Statistical significance:** Is the improvement real or a random variation?

Iterate Based on Real Usage

Analytics show actual behavior, not hypothetical preferences from research.

After launch, watch for:

- **Unexpected struggles:** Users having trouble where you didn't predict

- **Quick fixes:** Issues research didn't uncover
- **Refinement opportunities:** Patterns suggesting improvements

Close the Loop with Stakeholders

Report back on impact. Build credibility for the next cycle.

"Remember that research on admin license assignment? Here's the outcome:

- 33 percent task completion increase,
- 47 percent time reduction, and
- an estimated $500K retention impact."

This proves UX ROI: Research → strategy → design → shipping → measurable impact. The complete cycle.

Feed Insights into the Next Cycle

After measuring impact, reflect on what worked and what didn't.

- **What worked?** Successful patterns to repeat
- **What didn't?** Failures to learn from
- **What did we miss?** Opportunities discovered post-launch
- **What's next?** Strategic priorities for the upcoming cycle

This isn't failure—it's learning. Strategic UX is continuous improvement guided by evidence.

The strategic decision: Measurement isn't the endpoint. It's proof that strategic thinking drives results, which secures resources for continuous improvement.

Moving Forward

You now understand the complete Strategic UX Toolkit:

Phase 1 (Chapter 6): Assess context honestly: organizational maturity, EdTech constraints, and a realistic assessment of what's possible.

Phase 2 (Chapter 7): Select tools strategically: match confidence thresholds, context-driven choices, and communication artifacts to stakeholders.

Phase 3 (Chapter 8): Execute research and build buy-in: use your selected tools effectively with strategic sampling, rolling synthesis, and progressive stakeholder involvement.

Phase 4 (Chapter 9): Develop strategy and advocate for direction: translate findings into UX strategy and build consensus on which problems to pursue.

Phase 5 (Chapter 10): Design solutions and advocate for prioritization: task-based workflows for EdTech constraints, advocate for designed solutions, compromise strategically, and measure impact.

This isn't a rigid process to follow sequentially. It's your toolkit—a collection of tools and approaches you've selected based on your specific context. The same toolkit-building process leads to different tool selections depending on your reality. You've learned how to build your toolkit. Now the work continues as you apply it strategically.

The final chapter explores what comes next: how to start applying your toolkit in your organization, what to expect, and how to build momentum when you're working within constraints.

→ For complete tactical implementation—templates, filled examples, video walkthroughs, step-by-step processes—see *The Strategic UX Toolkit Playbook* (available at kellymorganux.com).

CONCLUSION

From Strategic Thinking to Strategic Action

Remember the pattern I described in the introduction?

A product leader discovers a framework at a conference. Gets energized. "This is what we need." Six months later, the enthusiasm has faded because the framework didn't deliver. The team concludes "formalized frameworks aren't worth it" and moves on.

You now understand why that happens.

It's not that the frameworks are bad. It's that EdTech constraints—immovable deadlines, locked-in users, seasonal access, three-user dynamics, technical debt, and regulatory requirements—break the assumptions those frameworks make.

But here's what you also understand now: You don't need to abandon frameworks. You need to build your own toolkit by selecting tools strategically based on your context.

What You've Learned

Part 1 showed you why standard frameworks fail in EdTech:

- EdTech's unique constraints (Chapter 1)
- The three-user dynamic that complicates every decision (Chapter 2)
- Six specific framework misalignments and their real costs (Chapter 3)
- Six principles for building your own toolkit (Chapter 4)

Part 2 taught you how to build the Strategic UX Toolkit for your specific context:

- The five-phase toolkit-building process (Chapter 5)
- How to assess your organizational and EdTech-specific context (Chapter 6)
- How to select research tools and artifacts strategically (Chapter 7)
- How to execute research fast while building stakeholder buy-in (Chapter 8)
- How to develop a strategy and advocate for direction (Chapter 9)
- How to design solutions and advocate for prioritization (Chapter 10)

This isn't another framework to follow rigidly. It's a way of thinking strategically about your constraints, selecting tools that fit your reality, and proving that user-centered work drives business results.

You've learned to build your own toolkit, not follow someone else's pre-built toolbox.

Starting Where You Are

You might be reading this as a founder building your first EdTech product. Or a UX lead joining an established company with twenty years of technical debt. Or a product manager trying to introduce research rigor to a team that's always worked on instinct.

Whatever your situation, you're probably wondering: "Where do I start?"

Start with an honest context assessment.

Before you plan any research, select any tools, or advocate for any changes—understand your reality.

Use the context assessment from Chapter 6:

- What's your UX maturity?
- How fixed is your roadmap?
- What's your technical reality?
- What's your sales cycle stage?
- Who controls adoption?
- What's your locked-in reality?
- When can you access users?

A little time spent on honest thinking about these questions will save you months of wasted effort applying tools that can't work in your reality.

Then select one tool differently than you would have before.

Don't try to transform your entire approach overnight. Pick the constraint that matters most right now and select one tool strategically:

If you're approaching a back-to-school launch: Use Chapter 7's fast-to-insight tools instead of comprehensive research methods that miss your window.

If stakeholders ignore research: Apply Chapter 8's progressive involvement techniques so they feel a sense of ownership instead of surprise.

If you're jumping straight from research to design: Use Chapter 9's UX strategy development to get directional buy-in before investing in detailed design work.

If you're designing a new feature: Use Chapter 10's task-based workflow mapping instead of feature-oriented design.

If you're advocating for UX resources: Use Chapter 9's maturity-calibrated advocacy instead of pushing approaches your organization isn't ready for.

One strategic tool selection. One better outcome. Build from there.

What to Expect

Let me be realistic about what happens when you start building your toolkit and applying strategic UX thinking in constrained EdTech environments.

It won't be easy.

You'll still face stakeholders who want to skip research because "we already know what users need." You'll still hit technical constraints that prevent ideal solutions. You'll still navigate political dynamics that delay decisions.

Strategic UX thinking doesn't eliminate constraints. It helps you select tools that work effectively within them.

It won't be instant.

You won't build your complete toolkit overnight. Building UX maturity takes time, proving research ROI takes shipped products that users love, and establishing credibility takes consistent results.

But each strategic tool selection compounds. Each successful research project builds trust, and each measured impact proves value—that's how your toolkit grows with each project.

It will be worth it.

When you select tools that fit your context, research drives decisions instead of sitting in Confluence.

When you involve stakeholders throughout, they advocate for solutions instead of blocking them.

When you design for complete workflows instead of disconnected features, adoption increases.

When you measure impact and close the loop, you secure resources for the next cycle.

That's strategic UX in action. That's your toolkit working.

When You Get Stuck

You will get stuck. Everyone does.

Stakeholders might push back on your tool selection, or you might struggle to access users when you need them. Technical debt could block the solutions users need, and organizational politics can derail even the best advocacy efforts.

When that happens, return to strategic questions:

"What's actually true about my situation?" Not what you wish were true, but what constraints you're actually working within.

"Given my reality, which tools get me to confident decisions fastest?" Not the most comprehensive tools, but the tools that fit your context.

"Who needs to feel ownership for this to succeed?" Not who you need permission from, but who needs to be involved throughout.

"Is this battle worth fighting, or should I compromise strategically?" Not every hill is worth dying on. Pick your battles.

"What can I prove with measurable impact?" Build credibility through results, not through perfectly executed frameworks.

Strategic thinking means asking the right questions for your specific context, gathering the critical information those questions reveal, and selecting tools that fit your reality.

Building Your Own Toolkit

Here's what I hope you take from this book:

Permission to adapt. You don't need to follow any framework with perfect fidelity. You need to understand your context and select tools strategically from whatever sources fit.

A process for building your toolkit. The five-phase approach gives you structured ways to evaluate your constraints, select tools that fit, execute them effectively, and prove their value.

Confidence to advocate. You now understand how to frame user needs in stakeholder language, compromise strategically, and prove impact. That's how research becomes influence.

Realistic expectations. Strategic UX in constrained environments is hard. But it's also how you build products that teachers actually use, students actually learn from, and administrators actually renew.

You have the knowledge. You have the toolkit-building process. You have examples from someone who's navigated these same constraints.

Now it's your turn to build your toolkit and apply strategic thinking in your specific EdTech context.

→ Continue your strategic UX journey:

For tactical implementation guides: Templates, filled examples, video walkthroughs, and step-by-step processes for using specific tools at *The Strategic UX Toolkit Playbook* (kellymorganux.com)

For free tool samples: Context Mapping Workbook, and Strategic User Interview Guide (kellymorganux.com)

For strategic UX insights: Blog articles (kellymorganux.com) on applying these principles and selecting tools for real EdTech challenges

The work continues. But now you have a strategic approach for building your toolkit that fits EdTech reality.

Go build something users love.

ACKNOWLEDGMENTS

 I want to thank my amazing editor, Julie Sykora, for not only being an incredible editor but also for feeling like a partner and cheerleader!

Big thanks to Val for creating an environment in which I could heal and get my confidence back, especially because you didn't even know that's what I needed.

I've had the opportunity to work with (and learn from) some fantastic women across companies. Lakan, Tara, Kristie, Kirsten, and Sam – thanks for being the people I can laugh (and occasionally cry) with, vent to, and share emojis and memes with. You've all definitely made things better in my life and work!

And most importantly, thank you to my husband, Corey, and kids. The fact that you see book chapters on my laptop screen and it seems so normal to you that I'm writing a book makes me feel like you have confidence in my ability to do anything, and also that you're used to me doing random things without really making an announcement about it – thanks for rolling with me through it all!

References, Further Reading and Recommended Resources

Frameworks and Methodologies

Christensen, Clayton M., et al. *Competing Against Luck: The Story of Innovation and Customer Choice*. Harper Business, 2016.

Design Council. "The Double Diamond: 15 Years On." Design Council, 2019, www.designcouncil.org.uk/our-work/skills-learning/tools-frameworks/framework-for-innovation-design-councils-evolved-double-diamond/.

Eyal, Nir. *Hooked: How to Build Habit-Forming Products*. Portfolio, 2014.

Fogg, BJ. "A Behavior Model for Persuasive Design." *Proceedings of the 4th International Conference on Persuasive Technology*, ACM, 2009.

Gothelf, Jeff, and Josh Seiden. *Lean UX: Designing Great Products with Agile Teams*. 3rd ed., O'Reilly Media, 2021.

Hall, Erika. *Just Enough Research*. 2nd ed., A Book Apart, 2019.

IDEO. "Design Thinking." IDEO Design Thinking, www.ideou.com/pages/design-thinking.

Knapp, Jake, et al. *Sprint: How to Solve Big Problems and Test New Ideas in Just Five Days.* Simon & Schuster, 2016.

Klein, Laura. *UX for Lean Startups: Faster, Smarter User Experience Research and Design.* O'Reilly Media, 2013.

Krug, Steve. *Don't Make Me Think, Revisited: A Common Sense Approach to Web Usability.* 3rd ed., New Riders, 2014.

---. *Rocket Surgery Made Easy: The Do-It-Yourself Guide to Finding and Fixing Usability Problems.* New Riders, 2010.

Marine, Larry, and Debbie Levitt. *Disruptive Research: Revolutionize How You and Your Organization Use UX Research to Understand, Innovate, and Compete.* Strategic UX Press, 2023.

Moesta, Bob. *Demand-Side Sales 101: Stop Selling and Help Your Customers Make Progress.* Lioncrest Publishing, 2020.

Norman, Don. *The Design of Everyday Things.* Revised and expanded ed., Basic Books, 2013.

Perri, Melissa. *Escaping the Build Trap: How Effective Product Management Creates Real Value.* O'Reilly Media, 2018.

Portigal, Steve. *Interviewing Users: How to Uncover Compelling Insights.* Rosenfeld Media, 2013.

Ries, Eric. *The Lean Startup: How Today's Entrepreneurs Use Continuous Innovation to Create Radically Successful Businesses.* Crown Business, 2011.

Torres, Teresa. *Continuous Discovery Habits: Discover Products that Create Customer Value and Business Value.* Product Talk LLC, 2021.

Design Principles and Usability

Cooper, Alan, et al. *About Face: The Essentials of Interaction Design*. 4th ed., Wiley, 2014.

Frost, Brad. *Atomic Design*. Brad Frost, 2016, atomicdesign.bradfrost.com.

Nielsen, Jakob, and Rolf Molich. "Heuristic Evaluation of User Interfaces." *Proceedings of the SIGCHI Conference on Human Factors in Computing Systems*, ACM, 1990, pp. 249-256.

Nielsen Norman Group. "10 Usability Heuristics for User Interface Design." Nielsen Norman Group, www.nngroup.com/articles/ten-usability-heuristics/.

Rosenfeld, Sophia V., and James A. Reston. *Object-Oriented UX: A Foundation for Designing Scalable, Maintainable Digital Systems*. Rosenfeld Media, 2020.

Product Management and Strategy

Blank, Steve. *The Four Steps to the Epiphany: Successful Strategies for Products that Win*. 5th ed., K&S Ranch, 2013.

Cagan, Marty. *Inspired: How to Create Tech Products Customers Love*. 2nd ed., Wiley, 2017.

---. *Empowered: Ordinary People, Extraordinary Products*. Wiley, 2020.

Cognitive Science and Learning

Clear, James. *Atomic Habits: An Easy & Proven Way to Build Good Habits & Break Bad Ones*. Avery, 2018.

Kahneman, Daniel. *Thinking, Fast and Slow*. Farrar, Straus and Giroux, 2011.

Thaler, Richard H., and Cass R. Sunstein. *Nudge: Improving Decisions About Health, Wealth, and Happiness*. Yale University Press, 2008.

EdTech-Specific Resources

For additional resources, templates, and tactical implementation guides specific to EdTech UX strategy, visit kellymorganux.com.

About the Author

Kelly Morgan, Ph.D., combines 15 years teaching high school chemistry and physics with 15+ years building UX functions at EdTech companies.

Her Ph.D. in innovative instructional technology focused on how cognitive science principles apply to educational technology design. Translation: she understands both how we learn and how to design tools that support that learning.

As a founding designer at multiple EdTech companies—government, non-profit, and for-profit—Kelly built UX functions from scratch while navigating educational technology's unique constraints: seasonal access to users, lock-in periods, three-user dynamics, and regulatory requirements that override design decisions.

Kelly now works as a fractional Strategic UX Partner, helping EdTech companies move from opinion-driven feature factories to evidence-based strategy. She specializes in untangling years of decisions while setting foundations teams never knew they needed (or didn't know how to build)—and she brings the perspective of someone who's been both the teacher using EdTech tools and the designer building them.

Learn more and access resources at kellymorganux.com